ONCE A DISTRICT OFFICER

Once a District Officer

KENNETH BRADLEY

MACMILLAN
London · Melbourne · Toronto

ST MARTIN'S PRESS
New York
1966

MACMILLAN AND COMPANY LIMITED
Little Essex Street London WC 2
also Bombay Calcutta Madras Melbourne

THE MACMILLAN COMPANY OF CANADA LIMITED
70 Bond Street Toronto 2

ST MARTIN'S PRESS INC
175 Fifth Avenue New York NY 10010

Library of Congress catalogue card no. 66–13730

PRINTED IN GREAT BRITAIN

Contents

List of Maps

What Next?

SOME time ago I was invited to write a short account of my life and work for a series of practical books intended to help young people to choose careers for themselves. The idea seemed to me preposterous and I said so. If any young man was so misguided as to try to follow in my footsteps, in no time at all he would find himself treading on stairs that are no longer there.

I spent the first twenty-two years of my working life in the Colonial Administrative Service, a career which no longer exists. Then, in 1948, I was asked by the Secretary of State to come home to London and start a professional journal for the Colonial Service, which was then being rebuilt after the disorganization of the war years. That, too, came to an end as the Empire and the Service dwindled. The last number of *Corona* was published in December 1962. Meanwhile, in 1953, I had become Director of the Imperial Institute in South Kensington. The old Institute had been built to celebrate the Golden Jubilee of the Queen Empress and the splendours of Victorian imperialism. Seventy years later the modern Commonwealth was emerging from what had been gloomily predicted in some quarters as the Decline and Fall of the British Empire. It was time to replace the Imperial Institute with a new Commonwealth Institute, designed to express the faith and the hopes of young nations looking, not at the past, but into the future.

The new Institute, with its blue glass walls and copper roof, is set like a great marquee by the entrance to Holland Park. It was opened by the Queen on 6th November 1962, and when the blueprints had been folded and filed away, this task was also done. The story of my working life could hardly serve as a practical guide for anyone.

Nor could anyone write a book on 'How to be an Administrator in Ten Easy Lessons'. Administration is an art, the art of dealing with people. It is sometimes a gift, and it is more often

caught than taught, like many of the best things of life, such as
getting religion or falling in love. It added up to much more than
the techniques of bureaucracy, the politics, economics, law and
finance of colonial government. As young District Officers we
were dealing with all kinds of people, with Chiefs and villagers,
with European farmers and Asian merchants, with missionaries
and tribesmen, with colleagues, senior and junior, and with teams
of experts. Only as we grew older did we become concerned with
what used to be called, rather pompously, 'matters of high policy'
and have to learn to be diplomatists and to understand the
sophistications of politics and politicians.

In our early years our dealings with people were largely
concerned with trying to do things for them or persuading them
to help themselves. We had to learn the rudiments of many
practical skills, to make earth dams and to sink wells, to make
roads of a sort, and timber bridges; first a little mud-brick school,
then a bigger one of kiln-fired bricks; first a dispensary, then a
cottage hospital. We were laying the foundations of little bits of
civilization in the wilderness and learning and teaching, teaching
all the time.

I tried a few tentative remarks about leadership, the acceptance
of responsibility and the art of delegation. They gave me the
creeps.

But temptation was tapping at the door. To open it only a
crack was to let memory in with a rush.

I remembered how, over the years, hard poverty had taught me
how to write for hard cash. That taskmaster is certainly no subject
for easy lessons. Nor is the gathering of many skills by the wayside.
In the war I had to learn something of how to be an Information
Officer, how to run a highly amateur broadcasting service in a
home-made studio, how to be an editor and a journalist. Later, in
West Africa, I reluctantly learned a little bit about being a
politician, and I was very bad at it. More recently, 'What next?'
has included working with architects and exhibition-designers,
and has been concerned with running an art gallery, a cinema, and
a theatre. There has also been a certain amount of lecturing. Most
interesting of all, I have had to learn how to fit teaching about the

Commonwealth into the complex of British education, as well as how to behave like an international civil servant. Even now, when our 'stately pleasure dome' stands complete, new ventures and experiments go on. Every day I ask myself 'What next?' and almost every day something new turns up.

Was there a story here? It must not be what in our family is called 'How we put the Drains in the Punjab, by an Old-Timer'. Nor was I prepared to compose a nostalgic Elegy in an Imperial Churchyard. The curfew tolls the knell of parting heyday? No.

Nevertheless, memory's foot was in the door. It would be such a pleasure to recall the past, to relive some of the never-to-be-forgotten moments. There was that golden, smoke-hazed evening when I was trying to catch a tiger-fish from a sandbank in the Luangwa River, and a dusty old elephant came down to bathe close by, neither of us at all concerned. There was the Durbar in Accra, where the Ashanti Chiefs went by under green and scarlet state umbrellas twelve feet or more across, wearing gold ornaments as big as golf balls and escorted by splendid men blowing deep blasts on trumpets made of old brown ivory. There were the jagged peaks of South Georgia, rising eight thousand feet out of a pale-green morning sea, hung between with glaciers, each one of which rested, far below, on a wall of deep blue ice.

The impractical, forbidden book began to shape itself in my shaving-mirror, in arguments with the bath taps, and polemics at breakfast-time directed at the patient back of a housecoat presiding over the toast and the coffee-pot. We began to remember together old jokes, old friends, old adventures for the book that must not be written.

Was there, perhaps, a pattern somewhere behind those memories which might give them more than a private significance? How did they fit into the context of their time and, since the story is still unfolding, into the context of the present?

Just about then a great deal of specious nonsense, or so it seemed to me, was being talked and written not only about British colonial administration and the work done by those who served it, but also about our background and education. We were mostly the younger sons of the professional middle class, and had been given a Sound Old-Fashioned Liberal Education in the Humanities at preparatory and public schools, ending with an arts degree from one of the older universities. The dreary old class enmities, to which a truce had apparently been called in the war years, were being revived for political purposes. The controversy about the public schools was also being hotted up by those who wanted to destroy them and they might, in their zeal, throw out the baby with the bathwater. Was there no place in a society which may not be so cynical and disillusioned as it pretends, for the moral certainties within a code which helped us, as they had helped our fathers? Are we living on our spiritual capital? Was there no place in a technological world for the amateur, trained for nothing but supposed to be ready for anything, who is the product of a liberal education? Whatever may now be said about the public schools, did they not produce three generations of men of the right type just when our country needed them most? I was tempted by these questions.

Bradleys have been dons, parsons or schoolmasters, or all three — and sometimes writers as well — for four hundred years. So had the ancestors of most of the District Officers in the Colonial Service. My mother, an army officer's widow at thirty-one, left with a pension of £150 a year and three small sons to educate, of whom I was the youngest, had managed somehow to send all three of us to preparatory and public schools, and two of us to Oxford. Most of my friends in the Service had similar, if not quite so poverty-stricken backgrounds. I was so typical as to be almost a perfect 'sample study' of the men who, for a hundred years, have gone out into the 'far-flung' to run the Empire and to help to turn it into the modern Commonwealth.

My grandfather had been a disciple of Dr. Arnold of Rugby and had himself, a century ago, helped to create one of the greatest of the public schools on the Arnold pattern. It was a surprise to me, when I looked him up in a *History of Marlborough College*,[1] to discover how radical that creation was. In its day it was a revolutionary answer to a practical problem — a population

[1] By A. G. Bradley (Murray, 1923).

bulge — and was in essence a leap into a democratic spread of education. This, perhaps, needs saying to a wider public than is reached by specialist treatises on educational methods or private histories of private schools.

I was, I dare say, an average product, but also a victim of the system. *Gaudeamus igitur* would be heavily qualified, I hope with detachment as well as gratitude.

Meanwhile it had also occurred to me that my own life-span, from 1904 to 1964, has coincided both in time and purpose not only with the life-span of the Colonial Service, but also with the change from Empire into Commonwealth. I started as a Cadet in Northern Rhodesia only some twenty-five years after the last Arab slave-trader had been driven out and when British administration was in its infancy. My Service life ended in the Gold Coast when that much more advanced and fascinating country was approaching self-government. Now I find myself working for more than twenty independent governments and caught up in the whole new conception of the Commonwealth of today and tomorrow. I have had to learn to adapt myself to continual change, trying to keep pace with new ideas, and always to look forward and not back. Here, too, in the context of our times, there might perhaps be something useful to say.

This would not be a 'rags to riches' saga, nor even a success story. Not for me the corridors of power, the cock's feathers of a colonial Governor. This would be the worm's-eye view, the story and the thoughts of an average man, written for average people.

In the Commonwealth itself there are today many opportunities for such ordinary men and women to go out and help in the enormous task of trying to narrow the gap between the 'have' and the 'have-not' countries. True, the modern adventurer has to have a specialist qualification, but not all of them need be scientists, doctors or engineers. There is plenty of room for the arts graduate with a diploma in one of the social sciences who wants to spend his life trying to help people to be happier and more useful citizens. We went out with authority, they go out as friends and servants. We went out to work *for* the people, they go out to work *with* them. Yet we, too, were their friends and soon had to learn to work with them, otherwise we could achieve nothing. We were starting a career, our successors go out on short-term contracts. Yet, specialist or not, the teacher or the agricultural expert may still have to treat the sick, to put up buildings or, when the rains come, to mend his road. The needs of Africa do not change with freedom.

The spirit which sent our forefathers out from this offshore island to the far horizons of the world, to the peaks of the Himalayas and to the South Pole, which colonized North America, Australia and New Zealand and spread British ideas, freedom under the law and parliamentary democracy, over half the world, is still very much alive. The qualities which made those achievements possible are still needed today in the places where they have always been most needed, things like enterprise, a taste for adventure, the habit of leadership, kindness, understanding, patience, compassion and guts.

Perhaps if I could recall what fun we all had in those long, dusty, lovely years in Africa, one or two of the younger generation might be tempted to go out there for a while and help. They would enjoy it as much as we did, though in a different way, and the rewards would be the same.

Then, of course, there is the Commonwealth itself. I have worked for it all my life. Its growth and change is the background of this story, as well as its meaning. Because I believe in people I believe in the Commonwealth, past, present and future, and I am ready to say so.

Any District Officer was, *ex officio*, a crusader of sorts, and in my sixties I am still at it. C. V. Wedgwood insists that any history must be written with passion. Mine would be. In any case, who can resist being asked to say what he thinks needs to be said about things he cares about? Not I. I took up my pen.

Today, as I read it through, I wonder. Memories are so beguiling. Old Chief Kapatamoyo with his long spear, who sat with me under the stars when I was young and watched Africa steal my heart; those two English girls I saw in Borneo only a year or two ago who were living in a longhouse helping the mothers with their babies. These and many others I have loved meeting again.

This is certainly not the book I was asked to write, and it may not serve any practical purpose at all. Perhaps all it has to say is that I have enjoyed my life and work, and still do.

CHAPTER I

The Rebel

IF, at the age of twenty-one it had occurred to me to ask myself, as I suppose everyone should, 'What do I want to be doing at twenty-six, thirty-six and forty-six?' I should doubtless have come up with some very odd answers. In those days, like many young people, I chiefly knew what I did not want. In a word, I did not want to be a typical Bradley. From earliest childhood I had been told that all Bradleys teach, or preach, or write, sometimes all three, and that none of them ever has any money or even the inclination to make any.

I did not want to go into the church or schoolmastering, as the family had been doing for four hundred years, nor, like my father, into the army. After three awful months in a shipping office in the City when I was eighteen, I did not want to go into business either. I had no ideas, only a series of rebellious inhibitions. Forty years later, I am beginning to wonder whether or not it is any good rebelling against one's heritage.

I knew all about the Bradleys, or thought I did, especially those who were famous in Oxford when I was young. There were also several family legends of dubious authenticity which were told to me as a boy, to inspire me, no doubt, although, like most parental efforts, they had the opposite effect to the one intended: one Bradley, John of York, ensign to King Henry VIII at the Field of the Cloth of Gold; Thomas, the chaplain on the scaffold with Charles I, King and Martyr; Jane, sister to Sarah Jennings, Duchess of Marlborough. All very picturesque, but they would have to be checked lest I be caught perpetuating even the harmless fictions of high ancestry. My wife cheerfully took over this particular exercise, as she enjoys facts and dates and people in history. Some of the legends, alas, had to go, but there emerged from these researches another kind of story and a continuing family pattern which seem to us to be more interesting.

Beginning with an Elizabethan, Dr. John Bradley of Cambridge, for the next four hundred years of the eleven generations of my direct ancestors, seven were dons, or schoolmasters or clergymen, and seven, although not the same seven, were second sons.

This is, perhaps, the pattern of many English families in the learned professions and the Services. During our own years in the Colonial Service we were surprised to encounter the sons and grandsons of so many of the great Victorian schoolmasters and clergymen with the same kind of family tradition. Benson, Storrs, Furse, Lloyd-Jones, Stubbs, and Tyndale-Biscoe spring to mind, and I dare say the files of the Indian Civil Service would turn up as many again.

The Bradleys seem to be fairly typical, in their ups and downs over the centuries, of the professional middle class which, unprivileged by land or wealth, has formed a tough, flexible, inconspicuous thread in the fabric of English life. Usually pious, and perhaps lacking in humour, they taught, preached and served. They represented a class which is apt to be obscured or forgotten now that our society is so often glibly classified in terms of income brackets and management and workers.

Dr. John Bradley went up to Magdalene College, Cambridge, in 1565, the year after Shakespeare and Marlowe were born. Doctor of Physic, B.A., 1568; M.A., 1572; Lic. Med., 1576; M.D., 1580; Proctor, 1579–1580. Then he died. I tremble to think what medicine he practised and taught. Surgery was for barbers. Cupping, bleeding, leeching, laudanum and arsenic, brimstone and treacle?

He came from Louth in Lincolnshire, where, towards the end of the Wars of the Roses, his family had a thriving wool business. His grandfather, Robert, in Louth; the elder son, Nicholas, strategically placed at Saltfleeton, down-river on the Lincolnshire coast, whence the wool-ships sailed for the Continent. The younger son, Thomas, was at the receiving end, a Merchant of the Staple, in Calais. In 1522 Robert and Nicholas died within days

B

of each other. One suspects the plague. Thomas, in Calais, who was our ancestor, inherited the business. He was nineteen.

This, so far as I know, was the last time any of the Bradleys had a thriving business of any kind. When I was up at Oxford I used to be asked if I were related to Denis Bradley of Balliol, a scion of the House of Bradley, the tailors and furriers. With only one suit, subfusc, and an assortment of 'Oxford bags', I had to say, alas, no.

Dr. John's son, Henry, came south to live and married a Reading girl. He was known as Henry Bradley of Wokingham. His second son, Thomas, in Stuart times, by going up to Exeter College in 1617 to read for Holy orders, began the long family connection with Oxford. Since then, except in the eighteenth century, there usually seem to have been one or more of us about the place. At times you could almost turn a stone and start a Bradley.[1]

In 1630 Thomas Bradley of Exeter became Rector of Ackworth and Castleford in Yorkshire, and Chaplain to King Charles I. There he married Frances, the daughter of John, Lord Savile of Pontefract, which is only three miles away. The Chaplain and his wife must have been there throughout the worst of the Civil War, almost within sound of the hurly-burly of the battles of Selby and Marston Moor. Adwalton Moor was on their doorstep. Pontefract Castle was besieged three times by the Roundheads and in the cauldrons of the armoury gold and silver were melted down and minted into siege pieces, Pontefract shillings, to pay the Royalist armies. When Charles moved his capital from York to Oxford in 1642, Thomas, as Chaplain to the King, came south with him and took the opportunity of acquiring a further degree, D.D., from his old college, Exeter.

Needless to say, I used to imagine Thomas, or rather myself in his person, for we all tend to identify ourselves with our more

[1] The sly shades of many of them on 'lissom, printless, clerical toe', in the ghostly garb of Stuart, Georgian and more recent times might well be encountered in University College (9), New College (3), Trinity (3), Magdalen (2), Balliol, Merton, Oriel, St. Edmund Hall, Worcester (1 each), and Somerville (2). Now a Bradley great-granddaughter has returned as Principal of St. Hilda's, the latest but, we hope, not the last of our dons.

romantic ancestors, clad in a long black gown and a square cap, with a pie-frill under my chin, standing on the scaffold with my King on that snowy day in January 1649, a sad study in black, white and scarlet. I know now that it was Juxon, Bishop of London, in the pie-frill. Nevertheless, Thomas was one of the King's Chaplains.

In fact, some time after 1642, perhaps when the war moved west, or perhaps to meet Queen Henrietta Maria, who landed in Yorkshire with munitions from France, Thomas had returned home to become a Prebendary of York. At the Restoration he was made a Canon of the Minster. After him, for two more generations, we are Thomas or Savile Bradley of Ackworth, educated at Oxford, and the canon's son in Holy orders.

For some reason, neither of the two eighteenth-century generations of Bradleys went to Oxford, but we more than made up for it in the nineteenth.

It was my great-grandfather, Charles, who restored the Oxford connection, and, indeed, the family pattern if not its fortunes, which were then at a very low ebb. I find his story moving because it shows how these things could be done even in the bad old days.

Charles was born at Wallingford in Berkshire in 1789, where his parents kept a Latin school in the village. They were so poor, he told my grandfather, that he could remember how during the Napoleonic Wars his mother used to cry and tell them that flour was so dear she could not make enough bread for her children.

In 1809 Charles, now twenty, obtained a degree as Master of Arts from Aberdeen University. The faded parchment tells us that he qualified in Greek Literature and Philosophy, and it describes him as Headmaster of Wallingford Grammar School. We do not know where he had learned his Greek and his philosophy, perhaps at home or at the Grammar School. It is astonishing that he should have been Headmaster of it, or even have been able to qualify for a M.A. degree at that age. The truth is that any respectably educated man could procure a degree from Aberdeen for a guinea. It was Dr. Johnson who remarked, 'The Rector of Aberdeen makes his fortune by degrees.'

Meantime, Charles entered himself at St. Edmund Hall to read for Holy orders. Somehow or other, while his elder brother kept the school, Charles got himself to Oxford and back, thirteen miles each way, three times a week. I hope he could afford a horse. There is no record of his having obtained an Oxford degree, but we do know that he was ordained deacon as 'Charles Bradley of St. Edmund Hall, Oxford' in 1812. His sermons were strongly, passionately evangelical and so popular that plans were considered for adding galleries to his church. In 1829 we find him installed as Vicar of St. James's, Clapham, where he remained for twenty-three years. There, again, he won a great reputation as a preacher. One man walked from London to Clapham each Sunday to hear him. We can find nothing to connect him with the 'Clapham Sect' of that period. We do, however, have a letter from the Bishop of Bath and Wells, written in 1825, regretting that he could not recommend him to Kensington Chapel 'not because of his character but his opinions'.

Charles was small and reputedly frail. He wrote copious letters of spiritual counsel to many learned and noble ladies, for the parson's study was the Victorian equivalent of the psychiatrist's couch. Over the years he had twenty-two children, thirteen by his first wife, Catherine Shepherd, nine by his second, the surely courageous Emma Linton, who was younger than the eldest of her thirteen stepchildren. He died at eighty-nine, having suffered the Bradley ill health all his life and still disliking noise! By that time he had over one hundred descendants. Some of them were already famous men and women, and need I say that twenty-five or more of them were dons, or schoolmasters, or clergymen, or were married to them, and that many of them were writers? Charles had, indeed, restored the Bradley pattern.

His family by his first wife included my grandfather, of whom we have always been very proud. He was the Very Reverend George Granville Bradley, D.D., C.V.O., Headmaster of Marlborough (1858–70), Master of University College, Oxford (1870–81), and Dean of Westminster (1881–1903). He was for a time Chaplain to Queen Victoria and he was known as 'the Good Dean'. The second and much younger family, Emma Linton's nine, included A. C. Bradley of Balliol, the Shakespearean critic

and Professor of Poetry at Oxford, and F. H. Bradley, O.M., of
Merton, the philosopher and author of *Appearance and Reality*.
The Bradleian at Marlborough, and a much-coveted Bradley
Fellowship in English at Balliol, commemorate those great days.
Small wonder that my tutors at Oxford looked somewhat askance
at my commoner's gown.

My grandfather died in 1903, just before I was born. His tomb
is in the Abbey, not far from that of the Unknown Soldier. He
was the fourth son and the ninth child of Charles's first family.
Yet somehow he managed to get a scholarship to Rugby when the
great Dr. Arnold was Headmaster. He then went up to University
College, Oxford, again with a scholarship, where he got a Double
First in Greats and a Fellowship in the same year, 1844. He returned to Rugby as an assistant master. Arnold had died in 1843.
My grandfather edited the only too well-known *Bradley's Arnold*,
a Latin prose book which is still in use more than a hundred years
later and still brings in welcome royalties to his descendants.
Then, in 1858, he was invited to become Headmaster of
Marlborough. He was only thirty-seven at the time, yet he was
one of the great headmasters of his age and one of the architects
of the modern public-school system. Having regarded him all my
life as an awesome pillar of the Victorian Establishment, I was
delighted to discover that in his thirties he was one of the radical
reformers who were imposing the Arnold pattern on the
educational system of the day.

The most obvious characteristics of the public-school system
were, as we all know, the prefectorial hierarchy, the worship of
team games, the over-emphasis on classical scholarship, a general
philistinism with regard to the fine arts, a highly conformist,
unenthusiastic and gentlemanly Christianity (the 'Public School
code with a kick in it'). To this were added 'nothing too much',
mens sana in corpore sano, and other shibboleths, as well as the
acceptance by the boys of discipline from each other through
fagging and prefectorial caning, and a Decalogue of unwritten
commandments, of which Rugby was the Sinai, and *Tom Brown's
School Days* the Testament. A new game with an oval football
was part of the mystique.

When I was at Wellington College, seventy-five years after Arnold's death, all of this, except the over-emphasis on classical scholarship, was still the accepted doctrine and practice. I absorbed it all, including most of the prejudices.

Arnold had not, as legend will have it, 'dreamed up' the public-school system in a fit of spontaneous inspiration and then codified it. He went to Rugby at the time of the Industrial Revolution. As one historian has said, 'For all his unworldly interests Arnold had a flair for a new market. He surveyed the social scene and he knew that a class of prosperous people was pressing forward to power and that their sons needed educating.'[1]

In the nineteenth century Arnold opened wide the doors of education to the sons of what were then quaintly termed 'the industrial and mercantile classes', just as now we see more doors being opened in the social revolution of the twentieth century. In the current dialogue of the class war this is worth repeating.

Like most English innovations, public schools on the Arnold pattern were an answer to a purely practical problem. In spite of continuing suspicion and opposition from the old guard, who expressed a pious dread that expansion would encourage 'a plutocratic element from the commercial and manufacturing centres', existing schools, like Rugby, were quickly enlarged to receive the 'bulge' of that day by the simple expedient of taking extra houses in the town. House prefects, house matches and house loyalties soon became part of the pattern.

When my grandfather's predecessor, the great Dr. Cotton, had himself left Rugby to become Headmaster of Marlborough in 1852, his new Board of Governors said they hoped he was not going to import the prefectorial system, organized games and other revolutionary Rugbeian notions into their school.

Marlborough had for centuries been a school for the sons of West-country clergymen and landed gentry. By all accounts a very wild, rough lot they were, bullying, poaching, 'squaling' (squirrelling) in their free time, fearing nothing under heaven but the brutalities of the bigger boys and the master's cane, living for

[1] Vivian Ogilvie, *The English Public School* (Batsford, 1957), quoted in *The Prefects* by Rupert Wilkinson (O.U.P., 1964).

the day when they would be big enough to take it out on a generation of smaller boys, their fags. Only the year before, 1851, had seen a Great Rebellion by the boys, barricades, a siege, fire and wholesale destruction of school property. Nevertheless, in his opening address, Dr. Cotton made his position clear. 'The Prefects are, and shall be so long as I am Head, the governors of this school. As soon as I see this impracticable, I shall resign.'[1] Prefects would mean a new kind of self-discipline among the boys, a salutary cure for the fear and hatred of all authority. Organized games were at first only a practical substitute for running wild and terrorizing the countryside.

In 1858 Dr. Cotton was about to sail for India to become Bishop of Calcutta and to found a college on the Arnold pattern in the Himalayas which still bears his name. It was he who suggested that my grandfather should succeed him at Marlborough.

By this time it was no longer revolutionary for the Headmaster to trust the boys or to take the Sixth into his confidence. They were already established in a position of power and responsibility. Place in the school conferred not a little social dignity. The Sixth was a tower of strength to him. They were able to regulate fagging and to try to stop the bullying. While still at school these boys were learning to feel the tug of the reins of authority.

Small wonder that a handful of men who had this schooling could keep the *Pax Britannica* right round the world over the teeming millions of the old Empire with justice and mercy as well as they did. The theory of Indirect Rule in colonial administration, that is to say, the delegation of power and responsibility to traditional rulers and Chiefs, instituted by Lord Lugard in Nigeria, was only the prefectorial system writ large, with, *mutatis mutandis*, the District Officers as masters, the Chiefs as prefects, and the tribesmen as the boys. The pattern fitted African tribal society well enough and was easily understood by Chiefs and people. At least one feature of the system, however, had unfortunate results. Just as the headmaster and the masters under him, by dealing with the boys through the prefects and by always being careful to bolster their authority, lost something of

[1] A. G. Bradley, *History of Marlborough College.*

their direct contact with the other boys, so District Officers sometimes came to be rather too remote from the ordinary people. At school it was 'not done' to appeal to a master against a prefect's decision. So any African would think twice before he complained to us about his Chief, and we would think twice before reversing a Chief's decision. We were, I think, more often respected than loved.

Grandfather's outstanding success as a headmaster was not repeated when he became Master of an Oxford College. There is a little story which, perhaps, shows us why.

On one occasion the Marlborough boys not only went poaching in Savernake Forest but sold their ill-gotten booty to poulterers in the village. At luncheon the little Headmaster rose in his place and said, 'I shall be in my study at 6.30, when I shall expect the culprits with the money.' Then he strode out and retired to wait. They came, and they laid their shillings before him, which he gathered up and promptly sent by a groom to the highly embarrassed owner of the Forest, the Marquess of Ailesbury. Some years later, with no success, grandfather tried to repeat this same disciplinary technique at University College, Oxford. The undergraduates had silently screwed up the door of the Dean's study, with the Dean inside. At Oxford, unlike Marlborough, nobody came to own up. Whereupon he sent the whole college down for the last ten days of term, and was thereafter much criticized. 'He would treat undergraduates as if they were schoolboys', they said. 'They are not at the University to obey but to learn to choose.'

Similarly, I feel that the Colonial Service, when it was nearing the end of its task, still tended to treat Africans 'as if they were schoolboys', adolescents not ready for real responsibility, which is the freedom to make mistakes. This was, perhaps, inevitable, just as it was inevitable that the Africans should, like undergraduates, react by asserting their freedom to choose.

It was a surprise to me to learn that my grandfather was a fine horseman and a crack shot. He was not too august to enjoy shooting on the range with the boys. A minor, and I may say a very Bradley touch, he was also a great pigeon fancier. The most distinguished clerical and metropolitan visitors to the school would be handed a basket of pigeons as they got into the railway carriage for London and asked to release them at some point or other along the line, regardless of chaos, dirt and droppings, feathers and furore.

I hardly like to mention that one of his innovations was the school cap, nowadays so familiar to us. Before his time schoolboys wore a flat-topped military type of hat with a glossy, stiff visor, easily cracked. After examining samples of these perishable objects, my grandfather sent to Oxford for his own tailor. Between them they devised the small, soft, close-fitting, indestructible 'button-caps' easily thrust into a pocket. For a hundred years they have had — shall we say? — their uses.

I wish I had known more about him when I was young. He would, I am sure, have been a great comfort to me. I wish, for instance, that when I had to build a little ten-bed hospital in Central Africa without any money, I had known how he had built the sanatorium at Marlborough. He needed £2,200, a large sum in those days. Friends of the school had collected only £600, so grandfather levied 10s. per term per boy for three years and thus found the rest of the money. How I scrounged the money for my hospital is a matter of unrecorded history.

He, too, was a small man who suffered, like his octogenarian father, from 'delicate health' It has become a family joke that in every generation those frail Bradleys are all but indestructible. 'You can't kill a Bradley', we say. My grandfather, it seems, concealed beneath a necessarily formidable exterior a wonderful sweetness of disposition, and it seems that he was greatly loved as well as admired. His lifelong friend, Tennyson, the Poet Laureate, said, 'I am sending my son not to Marlborough but to Bradley.'

Hugh, my father, was his second son. Like me, he did not want to be a schoolmaster, or a don, or a parson. Hugh was born at Marlborough in 1865, but by the time he was five his father was installed as Master of University College. Perhaps it was the highly academic confines of the Master's Lodgings in his school holidays, or the intellectual and spiritual pressures of the Deanery at Westminster, to which they moved when he was sixteen.

Perhaps it was having four clever sisters and a brother, all of whom were destined to be writers and who took themselves very seriously, to say nothing of twenty-one uncles and aunts and their offspring, some of whom were already brilliant academics or were married to them. For all or any of these reasons, my father decided that he did not want to conform to the family pattern or to go to Oxford at all. He wanted to become a soldier, and this he did, not without some trembling and a painful interview in his father's study.

He went to Sandhurst, then into the Gloucesters, and thence into the Indian Army and the Second Gurkhas. Also, he chose to marry his beautiful country cousin, my mother, whose complaint to the end of her long life was that she never had any education at all. Mother and her sisters were brought up in a country parsonage in the depths of Devonshire, under a series of horrifying German governesses, the kind who would pinch her under the table at luncheon as a signal that it was her turn to make a remark in German or French.

On one of his leaves, Hugh and his cousin Norah were married in Westminster Abbey and set off for India. Life in the cantonment was, by her account, exactly like the Kipling stories on which we were brought up. The regimental dinners, the balls, the subalterns sighing for a dance with the Captain's lovely wife (she was only eighteen), and the tennis tournaments in which, clad in a straw boater, a starched blouse with a man's high collar and skirts to her ankles, she shone, using a powerful underhand serve and a forehand drive which twenty years later her sons could only just return. There was the riding, the polo, the pig-sticking, big-game fishing and the tiger shoots. During our childhood a magnificent tiger skin glowered at us from a turn in the stair, his great head grinning from a low stool and his tail vanishing up to the picture rail. Mother would say, as she led us past him up to bed, 'Yes, dear, he sprang on to the shoulder of my elephant. I felt his horrid hot breath. Then your father shot him. No, not really frightened, there wasn't time.'

Three sons were born to them. Then, in 1906, when mother was in England waiting for Hugh to come home on leave, he died. An accident at polo, a chill, and that was that. Her only complaint of her Hugh was that he had been too deeply absorbed in his work. But then all wives of Bradleys have that to complain of.

Mother lived until she was eighty-nine, and for most of her life she was a widow. To have brought up her sons with no man to help her, with very little money and no ability to earn more, is a proud enough record, and this is an insufficient tribute to her innate capacity and the strength and sweetness of her character.

Mother had always been frightened of her learned in-laws at the Deanery, especially her intellectual and sophisticated sisters-in-law, who intimidated and seemed to patronize her. My own boyhood memories of the Bradley aunts are of alarming lunches in large houses in Westminster; silent butlers, ginger pudding ('so suitable'), which I still loathe; buying clothes at the Army and Navy stores before inevitable appointments with the dentist. Nevertheless, as the daughters of the Dean, they knew everyone in the educational world. They saw to it that Hugh's three boys were all sent to good preparatory schools. Afterwards we all went to Wellington College, where our education was paid for by a foundation, the income of which was devoted to paying the school fees of the sons of officers who had died.

I grew up seeing the Bradleys through mother's eyes. It was not until I had grown up and got to know them that I began to realize how much I had missed. When I began to come home on leaves from Africa and again went to lunch with the aunts (no more ginger pudding, but rich trifles, which I dislike equally, no matter how much sherry soaks the cake) they were no longer formidable. Each of the Bradley aunts deserves a book to herself. They were all beauties and all small, fair, frail and formidable. The most famous was Aunt Daisy, Margaret L. Woods, poet and novelist, married to the President of Trinity College, Oxford, afterwards Master of the Temple. Aunt Mabel married Sir Henry Birchenough, President of the British South Africa Company and Chairman of the Beit Trust. Aunt Nem, Emily Tennyson Murray Smith, wrote the definitive guide to Westminster Abbey. Their house, 40 Queen Anne's Gate, was bequeathed to the nation and is now the headquarters of the National Trust. She was an eccentric, not unlike Dane Chandos's 'Abbie', and a well-known social worker with advanced ideas. Aunt Posy, Rose M. Bradley, biographer and essayist, was given the O.B.E. for helping to found the W.A.A.C. in the First World War and was a Governor of the Greycoat School and Queen Anne's, Caversham. Aunt Mimi, the eldest, vanished to Arizona. We heard of four romantic marriages, but Mimi the Maverick did not, perhaps fortunately, take to her pen. I never knew her. Uncle Jack was A. G. Bradley, a professional writer of modest fame, a friend of Henry James, and a pillar of the famous Golf Club at Rye.

The aunts sympathized particularly with my early efforts to write, and to place what I had written. They had been up that hill themselves. Was I one of them? A Bradley after all? In spite of the handicaps? My schooldays had, alas, only confirmed me in my prejudices.

I was, I dare say, a typical average product of the system, but also, as I have said, its victim. Wellington was known as an 'Army' school. That is to say, it had been founded for the sons of army officers who would presumably become soldiers too; and even in peace-time most of the boys still went on to Woolwich or Sandhurst. I went there in 1917, during the First World War, when all its efforts were concentrated on producing officers. Most of the good masters were in the trenches or dead. Conditions were Spartan and the food, when the U-boats were starving the country, was atrocious and inadequate. I was on the much despised Classical side, what there was of it. Like most Bradleys, I was small and indifferent at games. I was easily mocked and mildly bullied. Everybody, and not least I, was astonished when I was made a prefect and almost immediately afterwards, head of my house. I remember to this day being sent for by the Headmaster, the great 'Daddy' Vaughan, and how he led me out across the green lawns in the summer sunshine, his gown billowing out behind him. He strode for miles, or so it seemed to me, until we came to a bench and sat down. I hoped, I dreaded, I knew what was coming. He said nothing for a long, long time. Nothing at all. I searched my soul, shamed by my inadequacies, clutching at resolve, hoping and praying that then and for ever I would be good. Good for something. A good prefect. Presently he told me briefly what he had come to say, and wished me luck. The silence had done its work as he knew it would.

I do not think I was a very good prefect. Nevertheless, I learned to exercise some responsibility and authority, which is the virtue of the system. I have repeated this story to show how, in my day, these things were presumed to be caught, not taught. Without ever hearing a word said about them, we were educated to accept leadership as a duty and a privilege and as our lot in life. The moral certainties of the 'code' were also caught, not taught. Most of us have found them a useful and reliable yardstick in after life.

Educationally, however, my last two years at Wellington were unfortunate. The war-time master still in charge of the Classical Upper Sixth reduced the glories of the poets and philosophers to the dust and dry bones of textual criticism, and what might have been an appreciation of beauty and wisdom to a dull, rebellious hatred of him and everything he tried to teach us. The classics ought to have been fun, but there was no fun at Wellington in my day. This was not because of the war — I was there until 1922 — but because it had not occurred to anybody that fun could be educationally valuable. We were not taken to visit factories or famous places, we were not even allowed into the local villages. We must be kept isolated from the world for which we were being prepared. High spirits were confined and recreation closely organized. We must learn discipline. Imagination was dangerous and we must be sent to bed tired. Perhaps I was at the wrong school at the wrong time. I was certainly not happy. Nevertheless, I have always been more than grateful for what Wellington did give me.

Having failed to win a scholarship to Oxford, I was put into a shipping office in the City for three months, and how I loathed it! Then it became possible for me to go up as a commoner. I went to Univ in 1922, hating the classics and almost totally uneducated in anything else. At Wellington, it is true, I had edited *The Wellingtonian* and written a rather sickening poem during my one blissful year in the Lower Sixth when I had been, by good luck, taught to love Homer and Virgil by an imaginative old master. In those days English literature, like geography, was

not a serious subject in sixth forms or at the university. Neither
at school nor at home was I ever encouraged to read poetry or
any good books, or to learn about painting or music, or even to
see serious plays. Nor did I want to. All that was vaguely lumped
together as 'English Classics', for holiday-tasks, like boring
old Dickens, Scott, and Thackeray. So I read Jeffrey Farnol,
W. J. Locke, and Kipling, and in the holidays off we went to see
Peg o' my Heart, Gilbert and Sullivan, and Dorothy Dickson, with
whom we were all in love, in her long series of musicals.

I came down from Oxford as I went up, a philistine, still packed
with prejudice. This was a very great pity, because Oxford in those
years was full of brilliant men. Scrymgeour-Wedderburn, now
Lord Dundee, and for a time my chairman at the Commonwealth
Institute, was President of the Union. Alan Lennox-Boyd, now
Lord Boyd, and Emlyn Williams were both at Christ Church, as
well as a shy young history scholar from Cornwall to whom one
was introduced as Rowse of the House.

Evelyn Waugh has written of those years at Oxford the fiction
of *Brideshead Revisited*, as well as, more recently, the facts of his own
life. He will be amused no doubt to hear a Bradley story of those
days. It seems that one of the aunts remembered the parents of
'the Waugh boys', and while deploring Alec's *Loom of Youth*, was
delighted when Evelyn published a serious study of Dante Gabriel
Rossetti. She bought several copies and gave us one for Christmas
1928, to encourage this bright young man. An order was left with
her bookseller that anything new from his pen was to be sent
round at once. Before long *Vile Bodies* (or was it *Decline and Fall?*)
appeared. The order was cancelled.

Everyman has his own Oxford. We said this to our own sons
in later years, adding that the important thing about the place is
that you leave it knowing how little you know. This, at least, I
had begun to glimpse.

For us at University (in spite of a consistently good record in
Schools it was known as 'the Pub in the High'), the world was
sharply divided into Athletes and Aesthetes. I could not aspire
to the one and had no wish to be identified with the other. Still
battered by the rigours of Wellington, I was content to remain

in obscurity, with one or two close friends, no clubs, working hard, rowing, playing golf at Frilford Heath and missing so much and so much. We did talk endlessly into the small hours about Life, and our horizons widened a little toward the politics and economics of the world we were soon to enter. No doubt we benefited somewhat from our marathon race through philosophy, which is the third part of P.P.E. Our minds, within the somewhat narrow, self-imposed limits, were being trained as useful, if inelegant, maids of all work. This is really all that mine has ever been from that day to this.

In the end I was pleased to get a safe Second in my Schools and was highly indignant when father's elder brother, A. G. Bradley, commiserated with me rather pettishly for not getting the First to which I had never aspired. It was he who had earlier written to mother to say that no Bradley who could not win a scholarship was worth sending to Oxford.

I may have spent too much time on the story of the Bradleys and my own education, but there is still that question to be answered: can a man break the pattern of his inheritance? We shall see. It has been a source of considerable amusement and some nodding of sage old Bradley heads that, although most of us have done our best since the First World War to break the pattern, as my father did, it still persists. There are two clergymen in the rising generation, one High Church, like Thomas Bradley, Chaplain to Charles I, and one Low, like great-grandfather Charles and the Dean himself. My half-brother (my mother married again in the First World War) owns and runs a preparatory school, another brother very happily joined him there to teach classics after he had retired from the Indian Civil Service. And I, well, for the last ten years or more I have been teaching, preaching and writing about the Commonwealth.

I hope, too, that these stories of the Bradleys are worth recording, because, in their ups and downs, they are so typical of our class, which is so thoroughly English and remarkable for its capacity to improvise, to adapt and, above all, to survive. The strength of the English social structure has long rested on its flexibility. The professional middle class has always gathered recruits both from the impoverished aristocracy and from an educated working class. It still does, and, as it is now absorbing more and more of the new professions in science, technology and management, it is more cheerful, larger and tougher than ever and, therefore, I suspect, it will continue to endure.

The public schools, created by the middle class a hundred years ago, more than made their contribution to our country. They succeeded in equipping England with several generations of men who, if no cleverer than the general run of people, were fortified by the moral certainties of the 'code' and an easy assumption of authority. Many of them thought of their lives in terms of service and a pension rather than of profit. They provided officers in two world wars and played a very great part in helping to build the old Empire and to create the modern Commonwealth out of it. With all their shortcomings they served us well.

At present the public-school system is under fire. It was developed to meet a need after the Industrial Revolution. Now the whole educational system of our country is being rapidly changed to meet the needs of our twentieth-century social and technological revolution. The public schools are changing, too, but, since they are very British, we can hope that, however revolutionary the changes may prove to be, the reformers will not, in fact, throw out the baby with the bathwater.

The aim of all liberal education, in every type of school, whether public or grammar or comprehensive, and in every university, is essentially the same, to produce what Confucius called the 'superior man', who 'bends like a bamboo before necessity, but does not break, adapting himself to society but keeping his integrity'. I hope I have not too unkindly described my own education at school and at Oxford. Did it enable me to do the many things I have had to do while actually qualifying me for none of them? Again, we shall see.

If there are people who say that a liberal education with such a purpose is irrelevant in a technological world which has little room for amateurs, I hope and believe they are wrong. As an amateur, unashamed, I have, since I left school, had a lot of fun. That fun in half a dozen fields is the burden of my story.

CHAPTER 2

Journey to Africa

WHEN I came down from Oxford in the summer of 1925 I knew what I did not want to do, and also that I certainly did not wish to sit for another examination as long as I lived. This ruled out both the Indian and the Home Civil Services, and the Diplomatic. There were, of course, other Services which were recruited not by competitive examination but by selection — the Sudan Civil, for example, but that, so they said, was 'a country of Blacks ruled by Blues'. They might have added 'and Brains', which seemed to rule me out on both counts.

So I put my name down with the Oxford Appointments Bureau and went home to see what turned up, as, I suppose, hundreds of newly fledged arts graduates do today. All through July and August offers came to our house in Guernsey by every morning's post — junior masterships in preparatory schools, 'promising openings' in everything from tea-broking to selling stockings and, I remember, at least one offer of a job with a publishing firm which I did not throw into the waste-paper basket and still had under my hesitant hand when the offer of a job in Palestine arrived.

The Colonial Office wanted an Administrative Officer for Palestine, which was then a British Mandated Territory. When I opened the letter I was sitting on a bench in our garden in the sun, waiting to go down the long cliff path, through the gorse and honeysuckle, to bathe off the rocks in Moulin Huet. Palestine might be fun, and I went with the family down that narrow path and into the shining, turbulent sea in a fine confusion of seagulls and surf, deserts, Bedouin and camels.

I wrote to the Colonial Office that night, and after several weeks of filling in forms and collecting references from my schoolmasters and dons, I was summoned to London for an interview with Major Furse.

The Colonial Service had not yet come into existence as a single Service under the Crown. Each colonial Government asked the Colonial Office to recruit what men it needed, and the Secretary of State for the Colonies selected them and appointed them to the Service of that particular Government. The oldest established Services were those of Ceylon and the Far East. In Africa the largest Service was that of Nigeria. I had barely heard of any of them. My knowledge of tropical Africa was limited to stories of David Livingstone, Lord Lugard and Cecil Rhodes. The age of heroes had barely ended, and the age of modern colonial administration, with its anthropologists, its technical experts and its theories of economic and political development, had not yet started. In later years the Colonial Service was to grow until, a generation later, it numbered about 15,000 men and women, belonging to almost every profession needed for the development of new countries: administrators, educationists, judges, lawyers, policemen, doctors, nurses, agriculturists, vets and scientists. It became, in the end, the largest and most highly trained multi-professional body ever yet formed with the sole purpose of spreading European civilization in the underdeveloped world. It began by bringing peace, the rule of law and ordered government to peoples who had not known them, and ended by abdicating from all its power and staying on to help those peoples, at their invitation, through the first years of the independent nationhood for which it had helped to equip them. The men and women of the Colonial Service did not build an Empire. Our ancestors had done that. They had established the *Pax Britannica* of which we were rightly proud, and in its shelter we and the Africans were free to begin, by trial and error, the long series of experiments which were to result in the evolution of the modern Commonwealth.

The Service existed, in fact if not in form, for little more than fifty years, and for thirty of them practically all its officers were chosen by Ralph Furse. He retired a few years ago with a knighthood and with the affection and admiration of thousands of men and women whose lives he had steered into adventurous and rewarding paths. But his greatest happiness must surely be knowing what his recruits have done for millions of people in so many far-off places.

I found Major Furse, as he then was, sitting in a small and dreary office in Whitehall, alone, behind a rather large desk. He was handsome, as a hawk is, and he had brown, crinkled hair and a kind smile. 'Well', he said, 'You can't go to Palestine — the job's already filled.' Then he gave me a long, cool and very perceptive look. 'Will you go to Northern Rhodesia?' he asked. 'Yes', I said, though I had barely heard of the place. 'Good. You'll do a three months' course and sail in January.' That was all, and I went home to Guernsey with my imagination groping among visions of palm-trees, black men and elephants, to look up Northern Rhodesia in our great *Times Atlas*.

To those who have practised or been subjected to the highly developed techniques of modern selection methods this little interview must appear to have been remarkably casual. So far as my one-word contribution to it was concerned, it certainly was. I took what was, after all, one of the most important decisions of my life without any thought at all, and my scalp can still tingle at the memory of it. My guardian angel's wings must have been arched about me. But Furse had already done the thinking. His methods of selection were, in fact, very far from casual, because every applicant had to supply not only complete details of his entire life from birth, but also references covering every stage of his education. Many people never even got as far as an interview, and others, when Furse was in any doubt, might have several with different people. It was all very carefully done, although some mistakes were made.

In those far-off days the Colonial Office was still new at the game, so far as Africa was concerned, and was chiefly concerned to recruit from the universities likely young men with a liberal education who would make good, sensible and sympathetic administrators. The day of the expert had not dawned and those of us who were not doctors, lawyers or engineers, were all amateurs. Even the training we were given before we sailed was little more than the embryo of the courses which were to be developed later. I spent three months in the old Imperial Institute (my guardian angel must have had a quiet, prophetic laugh at this!), learning about tropical products which did not grow in Northern Rhodesia; Mohammedan law, which did not run there; and the elements of government accounting, which were still too unreal to us to be absorbed. We also went to learn surveying on Red Hill Common. That did come in useful.

A few years later, as the Colonial Service grew, recruits were given a year's course at Oxford or Cambridge. They came out to Africa at the end of it well grounded not only in a relevant language and relevant law, but also with a basic knowledge of anthropology, the Lugard theory of Indirect Rule and other mysteries, and, above all, with sound, constructive ideas about the purposes of British colonial policy in terms of political, social and economic progress. The British are empiricists. They dislike theory and prefer to learn by experience, so that the Colonial Service grew in size, complexity, and quality in accordance with the need rather than according to any preconceived plan. And Furse and his colleagues in the recruiting department grew in stature, as everyone else seemed to do, with the Service that was being created.

I think that if Major Furse had been asked in the early twenties what kind of men he and his staff wanted for the Colonial Administrative Service, he would, having looked up at the ceiling and finding it empty of cherubim and seraphim or any angelic host, have settled for those qualities which the tough character-training of the boarding school and then the broad training of the mind provided by the older universities combined to foster. He wanted men who had been prefects and had come down from the university with at least a Second-class Honours Degree, preferably in Greats or the equivalent. He looked neither for brilliance — men with Firsts went into the Indian Civil Service anyway — nor for Blues, but he did want people who had learned at school the elements of leadership and to carry a little responsibility, and who had, at the university, learned to be sympathetic with the other man's point of view and yet to be detached and self-reliant. Especially he looked for men likely to have enough imagination to act on their own initiative and enough courage to carry the responsibility of doing so. 'Men of brains should be slaves', he said to us many years later when he was staying with us on a remote outstation in Northern Rhodesia. Then, seeing that we looked sufficiently startled, he added, 'Slaves of the men of character', and we were left, as he so often left us, gasping and looking for the twinkle in his eye, to do our own soul-searching. He looked for so much and had to be content with so much less.

A Service of amateur humanists was, as it turned out, admirably suited to the administration of unsophisticated peoples, but in the more politically advanced and complicated territories in later years, it did not provide quite all that was needed. We could have done with more brains and brilliance then, and many of us welcomed with considerable relief some of the men from the Indian Civil Service who came over to Africa to help us after the independence of India and Pakistan, where they were no longer needed.

On New Year's Day in 1926 I sailed for Cape Town. Five days later my fellow Northern Rhodesia Cadet (who is now Chief Justice of Malaysia) helped me to celebrate my twenty-second birthday in Madeira and we very nearly missed the boat as it hooted for its departure from Funchal Bay. From Cape Town we travelled northward by train for five hot and dusty days, up through the mountains on to the high veldt, across the Karoo; through the thorn-scrub and sand which fringes the Kalahari Desert, and up on to the Rhodesian plateau, where the grass was green with the early rains and the air washed clean and crisp. On the fifth day we crossed the bridge at the Victoria Falls and came to the hot little frontier town of Livingstone, which was then the capital of Northern Rhodesia.

In 1926 the Protectorate was only twenty-five years old. The emissaries of Cecil Rhodes had come north at the end of the century to make treaties with the tribes, and in 1901, under a Charter from the Crown, his British South Africa Company had set up two Protectorates, North-Eastern and North-Western Rhodesia. In 1911 these had been joined together into the Protectorate of Northern Rhodesia, which the Chartered Company continued to rule, at no profit to its shareholders, until 1924. Then

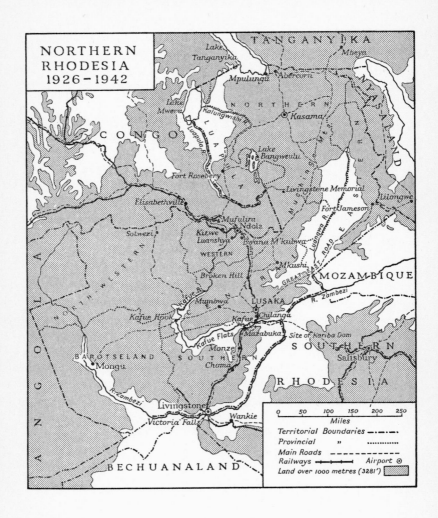

NORTHERN
RHODESIA
1926-1942

TANGANYIKA

Lake
Tanganyika   Mbeya

Mpulungu   Abercorn

Lake   Kasama
Mweru   Kalungwishi R.   NORTHERN

Luapula R.   LUAPULA

Lake
Bangweulu

CONGO

Fort Rosebery

Livingstone Memorial   Lilongwe

Elisabethville   Fort Jameson

Mufulira
Ndola

Solwezi   Kitwe   Bwana M'kubwa
Luanshya   Mkushi
WESTERN   MOZAMBIQUE

GREAT EAST ROAD

Broken Hill

NORTH WESTERN   Mumbwa   LUSAKA   R. Zambezi

Kafue R.   Chilanga
Kafue Hook
Kafue Flats   Mazabuka   Site of Kariba Dam

ANGOLA   BAROTSELAND   SOUTHERN   Monze   SOUTHERN

Mongu   Chuma   Salisbury

R. Zambezi   RHODESIA

Livingstone
Victoria Falls   Wankie

0   50   100   150   200   250
Miles
Territorial Boundaries —·—·—·
Provincial   ″   ············
Main Roads   — — — — —
Railways ⊢—⊢—⊢   Airport ⊙
Land over 1000 metres (3281′)

BECHUANALAND

the British Government, reluctant as always to add under-developed and therefore expensive territories to its imperial responsibilities, at last took over.

In those days there was no Copperbelt. In the tall forests only the dark buffalo moved and the cicadas shrilled for company in the empty silence. There was one copper mine at Bwana Mkubwa (long since worked out). Further south at Broken Hill zinc, lead and vanadium were being produced as they are today. That was all. There were Europeans farming green fields of maize and acres of yellow sunflowers alongside the only railway, which ran northward to the Congo. This was the beginning of what had been planned as a railway from Cape to Cairo. The main street of Lusaka is still called 'Cairo Road' and a popular brand of cigarettes is still, I hope, called 'C. to C.'. It is odd to reflect that the planners of the railway intended that it should chuff its way cheerfully 'C. to C.' through British territory all the way.

A thousand miles away from the railway a few other farmers had settled in the high country above the southern end of Lake Tanganyika, and there was another group growing tobacco at Fort Jameson, in the hills on the Nyasaland border. All the rest of this great country, twice as large as Britain, still lay, sunlit and remote, in the sleeping heart of Africa. There were few roads, and they were impassable in the rains, few cars, no aeroplanes, no refrigerators, and no radio. Away from the railway there were no visible signs of progress, except the missions and their schools, and, every hundred miles or so, neat little outstations where the District Commissioners ruled, alone but never lonely, over perhaps 50,000 people living along the streams and rivers, in the hills and in the forest.

Northern Rhodesia's budget was about £250,000 a year, which, they said, was roughly equivalent to the annual street-cleaning bill for the City of Glasgow. There were, as yet, no great pressures. These were soon to come with the opening up of the Copperbelt, but in 1926 life was still lived slowly and contentedly. 'The pace of Africa is the pace of the ox.' How often in moments of impatience and frustration were we to have that phrase handed to us by our elders!

Northward up Lake Tanganyika and on into Kenya you would have found all those thousands of miles of Africa very much the same as in Northern Rhodesia, though, here and there, more spectacular beauty. In Central Africa we had no Kilimanjaro floating like frozen cream in the high blue sky, no mountain-meadowed paradise like the Kenya Highlands, and no grass as green as that which grows round the bird-haunted fringes of Lake Victoria. Northern Rhodesia was much less romantic. It was, for the most part, plateau country of thin, iron-stemmed woodland and small plains through which lily-starred streams meandered to a distant swamp or sandy riverbed. Yet everywhere on this side of Africa you would have found much the same kind of white people living in much the same way. In those days all the Europeans, many of them settlers after the First World War, were still in spirit and often in fact pioneers. They were glad to be alive, for Passchendaele and the Somme had wiped out their friends. Most of them were hoping against hope and the economic probabilities to earn enough to give them a trip home, and to educate their children in England. The heat and the diseases, malaria and dysentery, poor food and tinned milk then dictated that no white child ought to stay in the tropics after the age of ten. They 'matured too early', they 'grew up like natives'. It was inconceivable to us then that a white child should boast, as they do nowadays, 'I am a Kenyan', or 'I am Zambian born, bred and educated. This is also *my* country and my home.'

To most Africans we white men were, in 1926, still a little strange and awesome. My wife has written of a tribe we visited, with our year-old son, and how the women gathered round for they had never seen a white child before. They thought him a very ugly colour and laughed and said so, much to her indignation. Millions were still living their remote and relatively well-adjusted tribal lives, accustomed by now at least to peace among themselves and freedom from slave raids. They were not yet very deeply infected by that acquisitiveness for possessions more elaborate than soap, salt or cloth, or a bicycle, the materialism which seems to be the life-blood as well as the disease of civilization. At least this, after forty years, is what memory suggests, but memories are not really to be trusted. Were not all our childhood summers fine and all our Christmasses white?

Africa was, indeed, no paradise. Fifty out of every hundred African children born were to die within two years; for two months before each harvest people starved; and all of them lived under the menace of witchcraft and in fear of the spirits which lived about them in the trees. As for us, well, we cursed the sun and the dust and the dirt, we lived almost entirely on scrawny chickens, we had malaria just as often as we had had colds in England, and we were always anxious about our children. But all our hardships and anxieties were concerned with the natural hazards of living in a harsh and untamed land. Sun, mosquitoes, tsetse fly, snakes and the other perils which beset all of us, black and white alike, were those of the age-old weapons with which Africa always has and always will defend herself. The protection against most of them has now been greatly strengthened, so that fewer babies die and more people live cleaner and more comfortable lives, but we have only to read the newspapers to know that progress has brought with it more complex and perhaps more dangerous evils which did not exist forty years ago when peace was new and politics were still unborn.

When we two Cadets in our new, though crumpled, tropical suits clambered down from that dirty train on to Livingstone's one hot platform, we knew nothing of all this. But there it all was, ahead of us, in those thousands of miles of Africa which were waiting to take, or perhaps to give us, the best years of our lives. We were in almost at the beginning, and the grass roots were waiting too for whatever we could do with them.

'You are going to be stationed at Fort Jameson', they said to me, and they pointed it out on a large, empty-looking map in one of the ant-eaten, iron-roofed ovens which were the headquarter offices of the Government. Fort Jameson lay about 300 miles to the east of us, where Northern Rhodesia, Nyasaland and Mozambique came together, and there seemed to be no road from here to there.

'The problem is', they said, 'how to get you there. If it were the dry season and you had had some experience, you could walk

across from Broken Hill in two weeks or so, but these rains are
the heaviest we have had for years and all the rivers will be in
flood. You or some of your porters might get drowned and you
would certainly get malaria. We don't want to lose you before
we've had our money's worth out of you, do we?'

The next most direct route would be to go down by train
through Bulawayo and Salisbury to Beira and then up into
Nyasaland, but unfortunately floods had broken the rail connection between Salisbury and Beira, so that route was also closed.
I would have to go further round still — Bulawayo–Mafeking–
Johannesburg–Lourenço Marques — then by sea to Beira, by
rail and river-steamer up to Blantyre in Nyasaland, and then by
road to Fort Jameson.

'But that would be a journey of over two thousand miles!' I
protested. 'How far is Fort Jameson from Blantyre?' 'Three
hundred miles, about the same as it is from Broken Hill, but
there is a road and a weekly mail lorry and you could do it in two
days. It should take you about four weeks in all, a bit longer but
a great deal safer than if you were to walk across. It's usually
quicker to walk in this part of Africa!'

In fact it would have been a great deal quicker and not much
more dangerous, because the journey in the end took seven weeks,
and I caught malaria at Beira and was in some peril of drowning
in Nyasaland.

However, all my luggage was relabelled, and there must have
been half a ton of it, as it contained all the china, cutlery, linen,
books, clothes, and camp equipment likely to be needed in the
next three years, and back I went over the same familiar railway
line, all the way down to South Africa again. Of that great
journey two bad memories persist. The engine which pulled the
train between Johannesburg and Lourenço Marques pushed an
open goods truck in front of it, and in it stood Africans in
handcuffs guarded by a soldier with a fixed bayonet. There was, the
Portuguese told me, a railway strike on, and those were the strike
leaders. 'Good way of preventing any train-wrecking', they said.

When the ship from Lourenço Marques docked at Beira, it
was unloaded by gangs of Africans roped together, waist to waist,

and supervised by overseers with hippo-hide whips. It was perhaps fortunate that I saw these ugly things, because one of our problems at Fort Jameson was to be the steady immigration into our already crowded District of thousands of people from across the Portuguese frontier. They came with terrible stories, and because we knew them to be at least partly true, we received the refugees as kindly as we could. In those days the Portuguese administration was indeed disgraceful.

The real excitement of the journey began when the up-country train from Beira reached the Zambezi, and we found that all the country to the north, including the southern end of the Nyasaland railway line, was flooded for miles and miles and miles. So the old wood-burning stern-wheeler did not ferry us across the Zambezi itself, but took us for a whole splendid day up through the flood-lands of the Shire River to Port Herald, where the hills begin. We thrashed our way under the flying sparks and smoke against the yellow flood, passing half-drowned villages huddled beneath banana trees, where naked children waved to us, and cheerful fishermen cast their nets in quiet pools among the restless reeds.

All the birds in Africa seemed to have gathered here, as though they had heard rumours of an Ark being built. Pelicans, ibis, geese, divers, and thousands and thousands of duck flighting across the sunset, when all the wide sky flamed and the water turned to gold. Later, in the hot dark, insects large and small came crowding so thickly to the lights on deck that to escape from them we had to go below and suffocate in our bunks under mosquito nets.

At Blantyre, up in the hills, where the air is crisp and scented by eucalyptus trees and a Scotch mist comes down in the evening, the mailbags and I and all my luggage were loaded on to an old 1915 Hupmobile with a canvas hood and a two-wheeled trailer. The driver was a cheerful African. The car was deplorable. We broke down fourteen times on the first day, but he always got us going again with a spanner and some pliers and bits of wire, and we covered about 150 miles. They were fun, those delays on the warm, red road, rich with the smell of the rain-soaked earth, the mud patterned with the footprints of barefoot people and the tracks of mysterious little animals. There always seemed to be people, too, for Nyasaland (unlike the rest of Central Africa) was even then thickly populated, and they all had time to stop for a chat and to help us push the car when it would not start. They laughed and sang and said nice things which I could not under-stand, and the babies on their mothers' backs were round-eyed and solemn and said nothing at all.

Then, west of Dedza, on the second morning, we hurtled down a long escarpment to the Litembwe River and came to a slithering and final stop. The bridge had been washed away. All but two of its great red-brick piers had gone, and the river swept past below us, yellow, swift and dangerous.

The local District Commissioner was standing on the bank looking very bad-tempered.

'You're new, aren't you?' he said, looking at my self-conscious terai hat and my spotless shorts.

'Yes. So what happens now?'

'So I will go back to Dedza and telegraph through to Fort Jameson — if the elephants haven't pulled the wires down again — and get them to send a lorry down.'

'And what do I do?'

'You get all the mails and all your kit across the river and wait.' He began to move away.

'How?'

He stopped short and turned round. 'Swim, of course, and don't lose any mailbags.' And he climbed into his car and left.

So, under the leadership of the driver, who was undefeated as ever, and with the help of twenty or so cheerful villagers, we unloaded every packing-case and swam all their precious contents and the mailbags across the flood in my brand-new, brown-and-white, tin camp bath. At least they did, and they never lost so much as a toothbrush or even got anything wet. Finally, as the swift night fell, I swam across myself, puffing and spluttering, while all my clothes were ferried over in the bath behind us.

Then Mr. George Banda appeared, a dignified, elderly man wear-ing a clean white robe. He raised his khaki sun-helmet and smiled.

'I am afraid', he said, in beautiful rolling Scots which assorted oddly with his cheerful black countenance, 'the lorry will no be here the nicht. I hope you will bide with me till it comes.'

So we walked up the road to a neat white house with a thatched roof, to which Mr. Banda, it seemed, had only recently retired after being Chief Clerk at Fort Jameson. He had come home to grow tobacco and to be near the Scottish Mission where he had been educated. His sitting-room was furnished with six deckchairs and a long row of assorted hats on pegs. He was altogether delightful, a most charming host, and because he (like the flooded villages, and the birds, and the blue hills of the Shire Highlands, and the driver and the broken bridge) was the first of his kind I had met, he and all those other things remain painted in my memory.

The lorry came late the next afternoon, driven by an elderly European settler from Fort Jameson, and we were on our way by sundown. Very late, we stopped in a cold, low-lying place where the elephant-grass grew ten feet tall and walled us in. He lit a small fire in the middle of the very narrow road, and when we had finished eating, he rolled himself up in a blanket and said, 'Good night. Keep the fire up if you happen to be awake. Bad place for lion and elephant, this Bua Valley', and he went to sleep.

I lay a long time, peering into the darkness, for there was no moon, listening to rustlings in the long grass behind our heads, wondering how I should feed the fire when our few sticks were burned. Nothing would have induced me to go and look for more out there in that lion-haunted dark. But in the end I fell asleep, and the small fire died, and no lions came, though one was killed there only a few weeks later and its carcass carried triumphantly into Fort Jameson draped over the bonnet of a car. It was near the Bua, too, that in the next dry season the mail car came fast round a bend and ran straight into the behind of a very big elephant. The elephant screamed with astonishment and fled, the car disintegrated, and the driver and his mate took to the treetops and stayed there until they were rescued.

And thus we came at last, with no such adventures, to Fort Jameson at the end of the seventh week.

'Can't think why you didn't walk', they said. 'You'd have been here in half the time. You young men are getting soft.'

CHAPTER 3

Grass Roots: Fort Jameson

FORT JAMESON was one of the oldest settlements in Northern Rhodesia. It had been built about twenty-five years earlier as the first capital of the old Protectorate of North-Eastern Rhodesia. It lay in a valley between two spurs of the border hills and it was a pretty little place, spaciously planned with red-brick houses spread along tree-lined, dusty roads. The church with a thatched roof and a pinnacled tower might have been copied from any one of a hundred small English parish churches. The tree-clad hills rose steeply on either side to a thousand feet or more, enfolding the little town and its golf course in their arms.

European settlers, Indian traders and missionaries of several nationalities and creeds had come into the District from Nyasaland on the heels of the first administrators and since the end of the First World War the number of settlers, mostly ex-soldiers and their families, had grown to several hundred. Some of them had been beguiled by advertisements in English newspapers of 'good land, situated midway between two railways'. So it was, but the advertisements had omitted to add that the railways were three hundred miles away in either direction. The settlers were, nevertheless, a cheerful lot and at that time, with rising tobacco prices, prosperous. They laughed at their own discomfiture and came into town on Saturdays to enjoy themselves.

In their wide hats, open shirts and khaki shorts, with little yellow bags of Boer tobacco tucked into their leather belts, they imported something of the frontiersman into the village peace. Nowadays I can never look at a good Western on the television without a faint nostalgia. But it was really the older men, the pioneers who had drifted up into this virgin country before 1914, that gave it this flavour. There was the younger son of an English county family who lived with his wife and daughter in a large, comfortable home on a plantation not far from town and kept open house for all the lonely young bachelors in the neighbourhood. There was the wiry old Pole who was a famous hunter of elephants and who had advertised for a wife in a Polish newspaper. Unfortunately the bride of his choice had lost her nerve and sent out a more venturesome friend instead, so that, when the bridegroom went down to Beira to meet the ship, a large dark girl, quite unlike the pretty blonde in his photograph, walked down the gangway. She turned out to be a formidable woman who terrified the Africans by keeping a tame leopard in the house and scandalized the matrons of Fort Jameson by larding her inadequate English with barrack-room adjectives picked up from her husband.

Then there was the old man, brother of an English High Court Judge, who lived disreputably on the Portuguese border and was said to drink methylated spirits when his smuggled whisky was in short supply. After a week-end in town his equally aged African wife used to take him home, laid neatly out on the floor of their ancient lorry, and care for him. Eventually, he died through mistakenly drinking a draught of cattle-dip out of a whisky bottle.

Much beloved was 'Mazoe Bill', a giant of a man who grew tobacco down in the Luangwa Valley and to whose employment Africans flocked from as far away as Tanganyika. He had led an 'army' from Southern Rhodesia against the Portuguese at the turn of the century. He had later traded, explored and hunted elephant all over Central Africa, and he had fought throughout the East African campaign in the First World War.

Most interesting, perhaps, though known to only a few of us because he never came into town, was the man who had 'gone native', living for years as an African in a remote corner of the District. He was said to have been to Oxford in his youth, and when he died his estate was found to consist of three beautiful sporting rifles and a box of well thumbed but carefully preserved volumes of Shakespeare, the poets and the Greek dramatists in Gilbert Murray's translations.

These were the eccentrics, who found even Fort Jameson too civilized for more than a nervous annual visit to the shops and the club bar. They liked to say loudly that the place had been ruined by the advent of white women with their tea parties, bridge parties, dinner parties and dinner jackets, tennis courts at the club, charity concerts, amateur theatricals, and a pantomime at Christmas as well as a children's party. There was a surprisingly large circulating library at the club, which smelt of damp and dust, but it was not much read as there was no provision for new books and everybody had long since read the old ones. The club secretary liked to tell all newcomers how the piano and the billiard table had both been manhandled by grunting, sweating, singing porters from the railhead at Blantyre before the war.

It is only fair to the present and to the future to confess that it would not have occurred to any of us to share any of our amenities with the Africans. There were many old-timers, good employers, who would have protected their beloved natives passionately from both education and Christianity. They were prepared to argue with the missionaries, who were otherwise their very good friends, that they were doing more harm than good except for their medical work. They quite sincerely thought that reading and writing would spread dangerous ideas, upset tribal and family disciplines, teach the people about the rights of the individual, as we have since come to call them, and thus breed a nasty race of rebels. They would become bad Africans trying to be bogus Europeans, belonging neither to their own people nor to ours. We soon learned not to argue when we were told, 'Never employ a mission boy. He is probably a rascal, fearing neither God nor the Devil.' These were experienced, kindly men. They liked their natives. They knew what was good for them. Kindness, justice, reason, firmness. Treat them like children. Aren't they happier than we are? Look at them, smiling, singing, no responsibilities — not a care in the world. We listened to this *ad nauseam* and held our peace.

Besides, who cared for so-called civilization? Were we not all in Africa to get away from it? One of our friends, a real old-timer, having at last made a small fortune in the tobacco boom, decided to go home. He had wandered north after the Boer War and could only remember London with horse-drawn buses, gaslight

and hansom cabs. He started off and got as far as Blantyre, and
then on to Beira. There, in that sleepy seaport, he saw some
hotels, electric light, and a few motor cars. Finally he took a long
look at the ship that was to carry him home, the carpets and
shining mirrors, the smart stewards, and the elegant passengers,
strangers all, and lost his nerve. He cancelled his passage then and
there and returned to his farm in the bush. That was Fort
Jameson as we knew it nearly forty years ago — full of character
and of characters.

The border hills ran north and south, sometimes gently folded
above sunlit valleys, sometimes soaring precipitously over deep
gorges where small rivers lay stilled in dark, rocky pools or
roared in hidden spate. To the west the hills ran down on to a
wide, thinly forested plateau, in some parts thick with clustered
villages, in others bright and orderly with the green tobacco
fields and thatched homesteads of the settlers. Elsewhere stretched
miles and miles of empty woodland. Still further to the west the
plateau fell away, down an arid escarpment to the steamy, deeply
forested Luangwa Valley where, as the Africans used to say, 'the
elephant is Governor', and man to this day lives out a precarious
co-existence with the wild.

Fort Jameson for me will always express Central Africa in all
its moods. It was so beautiful in spring-time when, under the
blazing heat of the October sun, all the young leaves uncurled,
orange and bronze and copper, and set the hills on fire. After
the first rains had fallen in November, the leaves turned green and
the woods were carpeted with little purple and yellow flowers,
like crocuses in an English park. The bush grew sinister as the
rains dragged on through February and March, with the elephant-
grass, ten feet tall, closing in on the roads and paths, and black
clouds lowering. In May and June the six months' drought began
with the stars brilliant in the rain-washed sky and brisk dawns
when the long grass hung, heavy with dew, across the paths. By
August all the grass had dried yellow and the bush fires began, so
that soon the whole country lay under a pall of smoke, black,
lifeless and hideous, waiting for the heat and the colour and the
renewed lust of spring.

D

As with the countryside, so with human beings. We white people developed a love-hate relationship with Africa. We loved its beauty and we hated its ugliness. We loved the freedom it gave us and we hated the prison of fear in which it enclosed our families — fear of blackwater fever, malaria, snakes, mosquitoes, ants, flies, spiders and other creepy-crawlies, most of which carried some dire threat in their armoury. We loved the sun but hated it when it became fierce and dangerous. We loved the adventure of living in the wilds but hated the predicaments we had to face when the thin veneer of civilization cracked, as when one's car broke down fifty miles from anywhere and one had no choice but to walk home for two days through rain and mud with no food or shelter on the way. Yet, on the whole we loved it and once Africa has caught your heart she never really lets it go.

The Africans, of course, knew no other country and no other life, but the same contrasts appeared in their ways of thinking and feeling and living: their gentleness to the young and reverence for the old contrasted with their cruelty to the outcast and the enemy; their gaiety of heart which was their shield against the ever-present fear of witchcraft and evil or revengeful spirits; their loyalty, courage and easily roused enthusiasm in such positive contrast to their helpless acceptance of hunger and disease.

There were, perhaps, for we could not count them accurately, about 100,000 Africans in the District, which was about as large as Wales. They belonged to four tribes. In the hills and in the country just to the west of them lived the Angoni.[1] They formed part of a famous warrior people who had once been under the influence of the Zulus and had acquired many of their qualities and customs. A hundred years before, they had migrated north-ward and had carried terror and devastation up through Nyasa-land far into East Africa. Most of them had finally settled in the country to the west of Lake Nyasa and for years they had spent their time raiding westward for slaves to sell to the Arabs on the lake. When the British came the Angoni fought one battle against them and then abandoned their military organization and

[1] Angoni means the Ngoni people, Ngoni being the adjective. Similarly with Achewa and Chewa, and other tribal names.

habits and settled down to admiring their cattle, watching their wives work, and sending their young men out all over southern Africa to be foremen and clerks, soldiers and policemen. They are still much in demand.

To the south and west of the Ngoni country lived the Achewa,[1] a peaceful, agricultural people who had survived in large numbers only because they had been spared by the Angoni to grow food for their *impis*.[2] The Angoni must have treated the Achewa very harshly to be so hated by them a quarter of a century later.

Below the escarpment, down in the Luangwa Valley, lay the beginning of those lands which had been the favourite hunting grounds of the Angoni and there, as over so much of Northern Rhodesia, only a few survivors had been left. On the Fort Jameson side of the river there were a few Akunda and a few Ansenga, living in small, isolated villages and only then beginning to revive either in numbers or in spirit.

I remember how, some years later, I came down into a far corner of the Luangwa Valley by a long day's march from the hills through uninhabited country. Our guide was an old man who had once gone with a raiding party by that route. Nobody else had used it since. We halted at noon by a stream where very old skulls and horns of roan and sable antelope could still be seen, half overgrown by bark, in the forks of the stunted trees.

'This is where the Angoni slept', said the old man, 'We had meat to eat that night.'

Towards evening we came in sight of the little isolated Kunda village which was our goal. The old man halted us while we were still hidden in the forest. Then he himself and two of his sons ran out into the sunlight, brandishing their shields and spears and crying '*Adza Kaluangwe!*', 'The hawk is coming!', which had been the old Ngoni war-cry. All the people of the village ran screaming into the woods beyond and when they came back later, rather sheepishly, they were very rude to the old man, who was still chuckling because his joke had been so successful. In the long African memory peace was still new, and the old terrors not yet deeply buried.

[1] Modern orthographists spell it *Acewa*.   [2] Regiments of warriors.

There had not, in fact, been very much change in the lives of those remote Kundu villages since they had last been raided by the Angoni nearly thirty years before, but the Achewa, up on the plateau, had already moved into a new world. Many of their young men were working either on the tobacco estates or, if they were more adventurous, far away in the mine at Broken Hill or in Southern Rhodesia or even in South Africa. Already to have travelled far and braved the perils and seen the wonders of the white man's world was for the young men replacing the blooding of their spears as a proof of manhood. For those who stayed at home there were mission schools in almost every village. But these, as I have said, were the only signs of progress to be seen, for the Government had no money and was as yet doing little except to keep law and order and collect enough hut tax to balance the budget.

There was no money to pay for development of any kind because in those days each British dependency was expected to pay its own way. With a budget of £250,000 a year the Northern Rhodesian Government could do little more than pay the salaries of its Civil Servants and could not afford to have very many of those. At Fort Jameson there were as yet no government schools for Africans — it was cheaper to pay small grants to the missions to help them to do the work — there was no agricultural station, no all-weather roads, only one doctor, with a small cottage hospital for Europeans and one for the Africans, who were just beginning to learn to accept European medicine.

This did not seem to us, then, to be so deplorable. After all, we did have a doctor, and a vet, a postmaster, a public works official, two policemen and no less than four Administrative Officers. Our roads were quite motorable in the dry season and the missions were giving most of the children some sort of elementary education. Fort Jameson was the best equipped and most advanced District in the country and we were proud of it.

All the officials, except my very new self, were of course members of the old Chartered Company Service. All those splendid men who had driven out the Arab slavers and pacified the warring tribes twenty-five years before had gone, but they had established a fine tradition of down-to-earth, hardworking administration. We, the new Administrative Officers, were expected in every District to spend at least 250 days a year under canvas, and to try and visit every village at least once a year. We had to do our travelling on bicycles or on foot with a string of porters. We had to read, write and speak at least one of the local languages and pass an examination in it, and we had to learn law and tribal custom. We knew our people and, as had always been the way of British administrators, we grew fond of them and defended them both against ill-treatment and exploitation by bad employers and their fellow Africans, and against the more unrealistic edicts of desk-bound bureaucrats at far-away headquarters.

Our official duties, in those early days, before Lugard's theory of Indirect Rule had been imported from West Africa and before there was any social and economic development in the tribal areas and Community Development had not been thought of, consisted of collecting taxes, punishing evildoers and listening to all the complaints and quarrels which the Chiefs and Elders had not been able to settle on their own. We mended roads as we went along, did our best to persuade the people to maintain the paths between their villages, to keep their huts in reasonable repair, and to carry the worst of their sick to hospital. The others we doctored as best we could with Epsom salts, quinine for endemic malaria, eye ointments and iodine.

None of us doubted our right to be there and none of the Africans questioned it. We knew that the British had rescued the people from great evils and that we were giving them a new and better life which already held within it the seeds of future civilization. The Angoni had never disputed the rights of conquest. 'You conquered us', they said. 'We are your men.' Most of the other tribes had not been conquered by the British but had themselves sought their protection and had not learned to regret it.

Nobody thought it was necessary to justify colonial rule and there was, as yet, very little discussion about long-term policy. Both the Government and its officials preferred to learn as they went along and only to formulate theories in the light of proved experience, which, in Central Africa, had been short. The British always distrusted the carefully worked-out theories preferred by the Belgians and the French because they seemed too inelastic and to leave less room for manœuvre in the interests of expediency when the inevitable crises came.

The administrators had no theories, but they did try to maintain all that was obviously best in the tribal structure and way of life, particularly the authority of the Chiefs and elders, and to see that the people were free to lead peaceful lives and were as contented as they could hope to be in a land where half the children died before they could walk and vengeful spirits lurked in every tree. Above all, we were supposed to be dispassionate and just and to try to win the trust, if not always the affection, of the people. We would have said then that it was the public-school code in action. We had not yet learned to apologize for it either to the Africans or to our fellow Englishmen. This attitude was typical of British administrators throughout the Empire, and it was probably one of the most important factors in the whole long, surprisingly smooth evolution of the modern Commonwealth.

This, then, was the land where I began to learn my trade in 1926 and these were the people who taught it to me.

CHAPTER 4

Apprenticeship: Fort Jameson

WHEN those kindly men in Livingstone had decided to send me on that marathon journey to Fort Jameson they had said, 'You'll like your District Commissioner, Cartmel Robinson.'

Nobody is more important in a young man's working life than his first boss, for by his example, good or bad, by the training he does or does not give, and by whether he cares or not, he can make or mar him.

They may even have thought it worth while to incur the very heavy cost of the journey in order to make sure that I should be given a good start by this particular man. However that may be, I could not have been more fortunate. Harold Cartmel Robinson, like so many of us, was a parson's son and he had won a choral scholarship to St. Paul's, and then gone on to Merton College, Oxford. He had joined the British South Africa Company's service before the war and had gone home to fight on the Western Front. He loved to tell how when he went home to join up, he leant forward and rested his hands on the official's desk.

'Stand up, you! Don't you know I'm a magistrate? Now then, what do you do in civilian life?'

'Please, sir, I'm a magistrate.'

When I first knew him he was in his thirties. No man in Northern Rhodesia was more respected or more loved, especially by the Africans, for he was not remote from them, and many called their children 'Lobisoni' after him. The younger men whom he had trained to work and think and care as he did, thought of themselves as 'Robinson's men'. He did not say very much to us. He thought it better to let us take in Africa through the pores and to learn by our mistakes. He gave us as much responsibility as he thought we could carry, and it was always greater than we realized. He was always ready to take the blame for our mistakes and to defend us against headquarters and all other critics. This, again, was the old code in action.

Cartmel always began by keeping our noses to the grindstone. 'There's the cashbook', he said to me on my first morning. 'Keep it balanced', and, 'There's the District map, see if you can copy it on a larger scale.' At the start of any job there is always that cashbook or its equivalent to be faced.

For days the cashbook refused to balance and the scratchings-out multiplied. Nor, for that matter, was the new map looking very tidy. There is at least one small blue lake on that old map of our small part of Central Africa which represents nothing but an ink-blot christened with a likely-sounding name. We had a sort of love-hate relationship, that cashbook and I, and all those dirty piles of money and the dog-eared vouchers. We had about an hour's close in-fighting every evening, but I enjoyed the fight and the moments of vicious triumph when that elusive sixpence had been tracked down and captured perhaps from the floor, and the book and the cash lay balanced and beaten before me.

One evening, when I was sitting, tired and hot, in that old office with its worn brick floor and its dirty white walls, stained with red dust and ravaged by white ants, Cartmel came in. He looked at my figures and all the scratchings-out and laughed. 'Good', he said, 'Now you can go out on *ulendo*.'

Ulendo is a word used in Central Africa for a *safari*, which is an East African term. It has a pleasant sound. Cartmel always sent his cadets out on *ulendo* almost at once because he knew that the true meaning of their work would only become a reality to them when they found themselves out in the bush, among the Africans and on their own, and also because this was the quickest and surest way to test their calibre.

'What do I do?' I asked.

'Collect all the tax you can. It's not coming in very well. Clean up the dirty villages and learn the language.'

In order to make sure that I did not make too many disastrous mistakes or take any foolish risks, he sent one of the District Officers out with me for the first two days, and gave me three of the best of the District Messengers to look after me and my twenty-two porters. The District Messengers were a force of trusted, hand-picked men, in part policemen, in part the eyes and ears of the District Commissioners. They wore smart blue uniforms and red fezzes and went unarmed. They were regarded by the people with an admirable mixture of awe and affection, much as we regard our local police in Britain. In order to make sure that I learned the language, which was Chinyanja, Cartmel removed from my entourage every man, except, mercifully, my cook, who talked any English at all, though, as I had learned the basic grammar and vocabulary on the voyage to Cape Town, I was not completely helpless. This was being thrown in at the deep end with a vengeance, but ignorance is bliss and I wandered off into the heart of Central Africa more than a little pleased with life.

The memories of that first *ulendo* are still vivid. I enjoyed myself hugely and committed every crime in the official book. Among other enormities I granted divorces to about fifty ill-treated or deserted wives, although I had as yet no jurisdiction as a magistrate, and I cleaned up dirty villages with a ruthless enthusiasm which infuriated everyone except the local school-master. But I did collect a lot of tax and I did come back full of confidence, speaking and understanding enough Chinyanja for working purposes. Happily, it is a simple language.

I related all my exploits to Cartmel with innocent enthusiasm. He did not blame me or discourage me, but when I had finished, he quietly and very clearly told me exactly where I had gone wrong. 'There are', he said among other things, 'two ways of cleaning up a dirty village. One is to be rude to the people and drive them to clean it up, as you did. The other is to explain to them why dirt is unhealthy and then to jolly them into doing the cleaning.' And then he smiled. I have never forgotten a word he said, I never made the same mistakes again and I stayed enthusiastic. Then he set about picking up the pieces of the damage which I had scattered all over the District and made certain that none of my scandalous activities ever reached the ears of headquarters.

Next time he sent me out he said, 'I want you to go round Chief Kapatamoyo's villages. He's a wise old man. Watch how he does it.'

Kapatamoyo lived in the valleys between the high hills. He had once commanded an *impi* of Ngoni warriors and was now very old and much loved and respected by his people. He was tall and thin, with a copper skin, high cheek-bones and beady eyes, and he always wore a dark-blue cloth about his shoulders and carried a very long spear.

He administered his own justice and although criminal jurisdiction had not yet been officially restored to the Chiefs, we would not have dreamed of stopping him. Nor would his people have thanked us if we had done so.

When Kapatamoyo sat in judgment on his stool of office with his Elders sitting round him on the ground, he seldom moved or spoke. He held the culprit and the witnesses with his eyes and they told him all the truth, which is more than they ever did to me in all my years. Then, when all had been said, he would gather his cloth round his thin old knees and give judgment. He could be hard on guilty people, when that seemed necessary, and fine them or ask me to have them jailed, but more often he was lenient, in the knowledge that no man would ever dare to commit the same crime again and risk being brought before him a second time. When no crime was involved, but rather some quarrel or misunderstanding, he was gentle and sympathetic and quoted tribal custom or from his own long experience to help in finding the solution. He and his people knew each other intimately and their relationship was lit by love. When he had given judgment they clapped their hands quietly to show acceptance and respect and went quietly away.

Now and then, in the evenings, Kapatamoyo would come and sit with me in the warmth of our great camp fire. He talked to me, as he had to so many other young Cadets who had been sent to him, like a father to his son. He spoke of the beliefs and customs of his people and about the cases he had tried during the day, explaining why he had hardened or softened his heart in giving judgment. Then he would recall his own youth and tell of the time when his people had come north across the Zambezi during an eclipse of the sun and how their *impis* had spread terror through the land. Young men, he said, as old men will, were not the same today — though it was true, he admitted, that some of them had recently killed a lion with their spears. In the long pauses of his quiet talking he would sit looking up at the moon floating over the misted hills and I would listen to the soft talk and laughter round the little fires outside his people's huts while Africa quietly laid her ancient spells upon me.

Yet even Kapatamoyo had his troubles. The 'King's peace' was at that time being much disturbed by a fanatical religious sect which preached that no one should be obeyed but God and that neither the Chiefs nor the Government had any rightful authority. Already one of its anarchical followers had set himself up as *Mwana Lesa*, 'the Son of God', and had murdered more than a hundred unpopular people for a consideration from their enemies by the simple process of baptizing them by total immersion in pools and rivers and holding them under until they drowned. He had been caught and hanged, but naturally the sect as a whole was not looked upon with a kindly eye. Its meetings were forbidden.

One day when I was sitting with old Kapatamoyo, word was brought to him that a prophet of the sect, called Zerubbabel, who was wearing a long white robe and carrying a shepherd's crook and was preaching dire sedition, had come into the District and was holding a big meeting at a village about ten miles away. 'Will you fetch me these people?' asked Kapatamoyo, 'I am too old to go myself.'

So off I went with my Messengers and thirty enthusiastic porters, and when we came near the village we saw at least three hundred people there. So we quietly surrounded the place and when I blew my whistle we all ran in upon them. None of us had any weapon more lethal than a fly-switch, but luckily none of the three hundred had their spears with them and they were taken by surprise. It was a great success, for we rounded up over two hundred of them and also found a large trunk which contained lists of thousands of names of adherents of the sect all over the country.

So we lined them up in a long column, and led by Zerubbabel, we all marched off to Kapatamoyo singing 'All things bright and beautiful' in full chorus. I do not remember feeling like a Spanish Inquisitor or having any qualms about religious persecution. As far as I was concerned these people were anarchists and anarchy against old Kapatamoyo, whom they loved, simply did not make sense. When I paraded them all in front of the old Chief they became frightened and ashamed.

Kapatamoyo thanked me and I felt like a heroic subaltern who had stormed the breach at Badajos — except that none of us had even a bruise. We had sung lustily for all that ten miles and until that moment we had all been as cheerful as we were tired, including Zerubbabel, who had been delighted to hear that I was a Christian too.

'And now', said Kapatamoyo, 'we will all rest. Tomorrow I take you in to see the D.C.'

The feelings of Mr. District Commissioner Robinson when old Kapatamoyo and young Bradley turned up at Fort Jameson a few days later with two hundred prisoners for our one small gaol can be well imagined, but, as Kapatamoyo had started the exploit, he was wisely allowed to finish it.

Kapatamoyo talked to them, as they sat in rows upon the ground. At first he was cold and frightening, then acid and more frightening still, and then he said, 'My people, you are foolish, but not wicked. You have walked many miles in the hot sun and your feet are tired. I have asked the D.C. to let you go home now, all except Zerubbabel, whom I do not want to see in my villages again. So go home and plant your fields and do not be foolish any more.'

And they all burst out chattering and laughing and clapped their hands and four of them came to borrow a litter on which to carry Kapatamoyo home because he was old and even more tired than they were.

Zerubbabel, who was really quite a nice old man, went to prison for a while and helped to keep the grass on the golf course cut.

During the first year Cartmel told me to organize an agricultural show for the Angoni and the Achewa. Such a thing had never been done before for the Africans and I had never been to an agricultural show in my life. The idea was strange to all of us. However, the old men who owned the cattle and the women who made pots and kept the chickens and knew every maize cob in the family grain-bins did all grasp the essential point that those who brought in the best cattle and the best pots, chickens and maize cobs would be given prizes.

We took over the local football field and built long, thatched sheds and cattle pens made of poles. Then we hung them about with plenty of gay bunting and waited anxiously for the Day, hoping that at least a few people would turn up.

From sun-up we were overwhelmed. Thousands of women came carrying baskets of produce on their heads, with squawking, red-faced chickens tied on to them upside down. The cattle came in unruly hundreds and six great carts with wheels made of slices cut from huge tree-trunks and drawn by fat red oxen with long horns. Apart from one petrifying moment when a black bull got loose and scattered the crowding women in a flurry of screams and a shower of spilt grain baskets, it was all a clamorous success, so great a success, in fact, that in the following year I was told to do it again.

By this time my fiancée had arrived from England and we had been married in the little thatched church with the pinnacled tower. So we did the next agricultural show together. This time we had no qualms and made more sheds and more cattle pens than ever and added, for good measure, a neat little model of a village for an example to the unhygienic. Alas, nobody came at all except the few who had won prizes the year before, and we were reduced to raiding our own hen-run to fill the rows of empty coops, and to collecting pots of grain from the wives of all the District Messengers.

This was a sad little story, but it did teach us some useful lessons. We were, I daresay, teaching them to be competitive, which they were not. We also learned not to be afraid of responsibility or new ideas or of learning strange skills; not to be too elated by initial success nor too discouraged by subsequent failure, and, less platitudinous but just as valuable, that the key to success in any scheme for African advancement was to provide a cash incentive for everyone concerned, a shilling in the hand being worth a hundred exhortations.

On another occasion years later, when foot-and-mouth disease was ravaging the cattle country and the herds had already eaten up all the grazing and there was no water and no rain expected for many weeks, the Administration and the Veterinary Department tried in vain to persuade the cattle-owners that small fat, well-cared-for herds, which survived, were better than large numbers of wasting and dying beasts. An old Chief explained their point of view to me. Cattle, which could be counted, were their capital, their wealth, their status symbol and far more valuable than their wives. 'Look, *Bwana*', he said, 'if you have many pounds you are rich. If this pound or that is dirty and torn, it is still a pound.'

It was thus that we served our apprenticeships in Africa, learning these and other elementary lessons in the art of creative administration, that positive combination of governing and teaching which was the function of the Colonial Service.

The teaching was still, in those days, empirical and rudimentary. It did not begin to emerge as a deliberate policy until the thirties, and it was not really fully developed into the most important arm of colonial government, equipped with specialists of all kinds, until the end of the Second World War when it was very nearly too late. In the twenties and thirties we thought we had all the time in the world. Was not the pace of Africa the pace of the ox? And consciously or unconsciously (no one had as yet codified the Four Freedoms) we were concerned only with adapting rudimentary civilization, as we knew it, in the context of local needs. There were far too few men and no money. So we were quickly taught to use initiative, to carry responsibility and, above all, how to make bricks without straw. What we achieved was very little by modern standards, but we did clear the ground and make a few grass roots sprout, and in the process we learned to be resourceful men.

Of greater personal importance, perhaps, was that during our first tour we Cadets learned what it meant to belong to a Service. 'Service' meant exactly that. We were committed to one of those professions where, as in the Church or in teaching, dedication is essential and brings its own reward. We were there to serve and not for profit, for there was none, unless you felt like going out to shoot a couple of elephant once a year on your game licence. We were absolutely forbidden to touch politics, such as they were, or to own land, or to engage in commerce, or to be involved in any way. In the Service the only spur was promotion with its promise of more pay and more allowances, a better house or a bigger station. We listened, unbelieving, to our seniors who grumbled that their expenses increased geometrically while their salaries grew arithmetically until we in our turn said the same thing to our juniors.

Yet, in spite of our perpetual overdrafts, we knew that we were very much happier than we would have been in that other world, so strange to us, where men were necessarily more concerned with cash and with getting on. In any Service the self-regarding have always been their own worst enemies and the least efficient officers. Most of us were far too busy and too deeply and happily involved to waste time worrying about the future. When your work is your life, there is no overtime. The work itself dictates where and how it is done. Even our Sunday picnics tended to be expeditions to see how a new bridge or road was getting on.

The discipline, in its widest sense, imposed by the Colonial Service did not of itself cause us any problems because we had been so well conditioned for it by background and education. Some years ago I wrote a little book called *The Colonial Service as a Career*[1] in which I described it like this: 'The Service imposes its own discipline on its members through the very qualities which the life and work demand . . . there are few detailed regulations other than those required to ensure the smooth working of any organization. You are not fettered in the detail of your conduct, either at work or in your private life. All the discipline of that kind is implicit and based on the assumption that you are proud of the Service and its traditions and will not betray them. From the start you are treated as a responsible human being, not as a cipher, and those in whose charge you find yourself will be your friends, if you will let them. In fact, you may be rather bewildered by your welcome and the ease of your relationships; you may even wonder whether there is enough discipline — but you will soon

[1] H.M.S.O., 1950, p. 24.

begin to see the underlying assumptions and all that they imply.
You will very soon discover that you are subject to the finest, the
most demanding and, on occasions, the most ruthless of disciplines,
self-discipline . . . and you will also find out for yourself whether
you measure up to the standards it demands.' There is nothing I
want to add to that.

In July 1928 it was time for us to go on leave. So we sold most
of our few battered possessions to pay off the grocery bills, packed
our nine-month-old son in a carry-cot, which was, in fact, the
wicker lining of that same old brown-and-white tin bath, and
went down to Beira to take ship for London. For two and a half
years we had been cut off from the world, for there was no radio
and our newspapers had taken six weeks to reach us. None of us
had really been conscious of our isolation. We had all lived a close
and intimate community life, full of interest and recurring drama.
We had been remote from the beginnings of the Copperbelt and
the changes which were taking place all over Africa and all but
oblivious of the great world beyond. We had changed, of course,
but we did not know it, and I can still remember our own shock
at meeting 'civilization' again. We boarded the liner at Beira in
the evening and, dusty and hot, I stood, dressed in khaki shirt and
shorts, on the gallery above the first-class dining-saloon, looking
down on people in black dinner jackets and pretty dresses, being
waited on by white stewards in the brilliance of electric light. It
was like some terrifying Aladdin's cave. How well we understood
our friend, the old-timer, who had turned tail and fled back to the
bush. The cabin steward grinned and asked us if we would like
an apple with our morning tea. An apple? Wouldn't we just!

At Cape Town we were surprised and delighted to find that
my salary, along with everyone else's, had been raised, in my case
from £375 to £450 a year. We were rich!

At Southampton we made the taxi-driver stop outside the docks
so that we could feast our eyes on a small square patch of muni-
cipal English grass. It was the first truly green grass we had seen
for two and a half years.

CHAPTER 5

District Officer: Mazabuka

WHILE we had been in Africa the Colonial Office had come to two important decisions about the Colonial Administrative Service: first, that a three months' course at the Imperial Institute was quite inadequate for the training of its recruits and, second, that they must build a wider bridge of understanding between the Office in Whitehall and the Service itself, the men on the spot.

The first decision led, in 1928, to the establishment of postgraduate courses at Oxford and Cambridge, and later in London as well, for administrative Cadets. The courses lasted for a full academic year and the Cadets at Oxford called themselves 'the Hartebeestes'. They had a wonderful time, but they also learned a great deal more than we had at the Imperial Institute. The introduction of these courses, which were improved and multiplied as the years went by, marked the beginning of professionalism and the recognition that colonial administration was a highly skilled art. The day of the amateur was passing. Soon the young, trained men began to rise in the Service, and policy to be formulated more explicitly as the education of the colonial peoples to take a larger part in governing themselves, still within the context of 'plenty of time', and of Indirect Rule, with all its implications of political, social and economic development.

The second decision, to improve the liaison between Whitehall and the Service at a lower level than the despatches exchanged between the Secretary of State and the Governors, led to the setting up of a system of secondments. Young men were to be brought home from the colonies to serve for a year or two in Whitehall and, what seemed more important to us, every man in the Colonial Office was to be given during his career one or two periods of secondment to a colony. This system was kept in operation more or less continuously for thirty-five years and did much to keep the Colonial Office in sympathetic touch with the Service and to maintain a human and understanding relationship between us. It is a great help to be able to put a face to the man you are writing to, and also to know what he will or will not be likely to do with any given problem you are submitting to him. The Service people on secondment to the Colonial Office were nicknamed 'Beachcombers'.

I was one of the lucky ones because I was offered a chance to be one of the earliest Beachcombers on that first leave of ours in 1928. Not yet having served at Headquarters in Africa and never having written a minute or drafted a despatch in my life, I had no relevant qualifications or experience whatever. I think I was only given the appointment because my wife sent me up to the corridors of Downing Street on the same morning that we heard of the vacancy. Had not, she said, Uncle Henry Birchenough once advised me never to miss an opportunity? Two years in London with a proper English nanny and access to a real library sounded heaven to her, so I went up and asked for the job in person. How to live in London on £750 a year (including a special allowance of £300) would be answered in due course.

Unfortunately, the Colonial Office did not feel that it would be at all fitting to post me to the Central African Department when I might make impertinent criticisms of my own Governor's despatches, so I spent six months grappling in total ignorance with the irrelevant problems of Transjordan, Iraq and Palestine. My chief memories are of quantities of railway lines required for the Kantara–Rafa railway which were always getting lost. In the files there were romantic reports of Bedouin raids into British territory, and on the bookshelf an unexpurgated edition of Burton's *Arabian Nights*, which I read from cover to cover in long, idle moments. It was, I was told, one of several books left there by T. E. Lawrence, who had, for a brief, unhappy period, occupied my seat. I am certain that I contributed nothing to policy in the Middle East or anywhere else and that 'Beachcomber' was a very apt nickname, but I *was* probably the first man ever to wear a pullover and a homburg hat to the Office in Whitehall. Young Anthony Eden had also eschewed the bowler, so I was in good company, though his homburg was black and smart and mine was brown and not smart at all. When I went down to have tea with the Central African Department I did tell them lion stories. It was kind of the Colonial Office to have me, and for me that winter in London had several important consequences. Driven by the sheer necessity of having no shilling in the housekeeping money for gas one cold Saturday night (we borrowed one from the Bobby on the beat in Old Chelsea), I began to teach myself to write, of which more later. Officially I would now be marked out for a headquarters appointment after my return to Africa, and thus, we hoped, destined for a much more varied career than I had ever thought of, and I have had friends in the Colonial Office ever since.

We sailed for Cape Town in June 1929 and travelled north from there through one of the coldest winters South Africans could remember. Blizzards were sweeping across the stark desert kopjes of the Karoo, the train was unheated and our son, now eighteen months old, was cutting his molars and cried dismally all the way. It was pleasant to return to the warm, unclouded sunlight of Rhodesia. It was pleasant, too, to be sent to Mumbwa, a small two-man outstation about a hundred miles west of Lusaka.

We were there, however, for only a few months before I was transferred to take charge, this time, of another two-man station called Mkushi, to the east of Broken Hill. Then, after only three months there, I was sent for to go and work in the Secretariat, the headquarters of the administration in Livingstone. So we were continually unpacking all our possessions and repacking them and loading them on to trucks and trains. When we reached Livingstone, to set up home for the third time in nine months, some of them were in a very battered state and our small stock of china was much depleted. But it was good training for us because during our twenty-two years in the Colonial Service we were to live in seventeen different houses. We used to say to each other, 'Never plant roses, because as soon as you do, you'll be transferred.' Our wives used to say that no sooner had they lengthened or shortened the curtains to fit one house than they were whisked off to another, and had it all to do again.

It was also exciting to be given my own District, at Mkushi, when I was only twenty-six. I had not hoped to have one for many years. It was equally exciting to be given a Secretariat appointment. This might be the bottom rung on a ladder to the stars and for a while ambition raised her seductive little head, holding up the prospect of a Governor's sword and cock's feathers in years to come. On such occasions, when we who had been too young for the First World War, took three steps up (and slipped back two), we were never allowed to forget that we were filling the gap left by better men than we, who had died in the trenches in Flanders. This has been true of all English public life for half a century. In those days 'Where have all the young men gone?' was not a song, but a practical question. I once heard Tubby Clayton say, leaning forward in the pulpit at St. Mary's, Oxford, so that the candlelight was caught in his thick spectacles, 'I was talking yesterday to the other man of my year at Magdalen who survived the war.'

In Northern Rhodesia we had also been caught up in a man-power shortage which was consequent upon the discovery of copper. The great mines on the Copperbelt were being opened up. Europeans and Africans by the thousands were pouring into the forest along the Congo border. Townships were springing up and roads and railways being built and the Government had somehow to provide District Officers, doctors and surveyors, as well as postmasters, policemen and all kinds of other officials whom they did not possess and most of whom, when recruited in London or South Africa, would have to be trained before being sent to us. The result was that the more experienced District Officers were needed on the Copperbelt and fortunate youngsters like myself had to take over the outstations. Similarly, the Secretariat and the headquarters departments found themselves overwhelmed with work. I was the only District Officer with Colonial Office experience, so, grasping at straws, they wrenched me from my new little kingdom and sent for me.

From then on, for the next twelve years, I was, like many others, to lead a shuttlecock existence between the Districts and headquarters.

As new recruits streamed out from the Oxford and Cambridge courses, we became a very young Service, and by 1938 some of the most important Districts, including the new towns on the Copperbelt, were being administered by men in their early thirties.

Between 1930 and 1939 I had five years' experience as a District Officer, but mercifully we were spared the Copperbelt. I had not come to darkest Africa to lose myself in what is now hideously called an industrial conurbation. First, in 1932, we went to Mazabuka for two years, during the second of which I became District Commissioner. Mazabuka was the centre of a big District on the railway line south of the Kafue River. The Europeans grew maize and tobacco and bred cattle for the hungry Copperbelt. The Africans included many maize farmers, too, and some of the most progressive as well as some of the most primitive people in Central Africa. Some of the problems were not unlike those of Fort Jameson, with the same segregation of Africans in big Reserves and the same perennial labour troubles on the European estates. But there the resemblance ended.

Mazabuka, in those days, was an ugly little township of one dusty street built alongside the railway under a low, rocky ridge. It was very hot. Near the town a little stream, dry except in the rains, called the Nakambala, ran under the single railway track, through a culvert. Ten miles further north another stream also passed under the line and it was called the Mazabuka. When the railway was being built the engineers made a siding at every tenth mile and painted a name-board for it. Unfortunately, the name-boards of the Nakambala and Mazabuka sidings had been mistakenly switched round. So Mazabuka had been wrongly named and now, thirty years later, it still looked ashamed of the fact.

On the ridge above the town we had a nine-hole golf course and from its little thatched clubhouse there was a tremendous view to the west, far out across the Kafue Flats. The Kafue River starts on the Congo border on the Copperbelt and flows for a hundred miles or so to the south-west before making a great bend to the south and east on its long journey to its meeting with the lower Zambezi. The country within this bend, known as the

'Hook of the Kafue', was in the Mumbwa District. Below the bend and on its eastward course towards the hills of the Zambezi escarpment, the river meanders across a vast grassy plain about 50 miles long and 20 miles wide, which it floods each rainy season. It is this plain which is called the Kafue Flats. Seen from our little clubhouse it looked like the sea, stretching green and blue, with here and there the silver gleam of sunlit water, to a flat horizon with one or two isolated hills standing along it. Towards the end of the dry winter, when the grass fires were burning, plumes of dark smoke on this far horizon might have been ships passing below the rim of the world.

Up at the golf club in the evenings we used to sit over our whiskies and soda and dream about the future of the Flats. The veterinary experts saw them drained and poldered, teeming with vast herds of fat cattle, instead of the buffalo and lechwe antelope which now roamed there when the floods went down. The agricultural experts saw them drained and poldered, too, populated not by cattle, but by farmers growing rice and vegetables, instead of the few scattered settlements of the stone-age Batwa people who lived there now.

Mazabuka was full of such experts because not far away from the town lay the headquarters of the Agricultural and Veterinary Departments, which shared a big, combined research station, and also the headquarters of the African Education Department with its teacher-training school and a sizeable African hospital. But because there was no money in those days for costly economic development, our dreams for reclaiming the Flats remained only dreams. Now, however, those of the agriculturists may have come true. Thirty years later the far-sighted directors of the Rhodesian Selection Trust Group of copper mines have financed an experimental scheme for creating poldered and drained small-holdings on the Flats. If the experiment is successful the Flats will one day be farmed by thousands of African smallholders growing food for the ever-increasing population of their country. There are plans, too, for the large-scale production of sugar on the lighter soils round the edges of the plain. But where the first small-holdings lie, we, in our day, used to walk out over the caked black soil and young green grass of the Flats in the early rains, when the sunset flamed on the horizon under black flat-bottomed clouds, and shoot sandgrouse and knob-nosed geese.

The Batwa people had prognathous heads and, because they lived in dug-out canoes and seldom walked, enormous shoulders and little legs like bent twigs. They lived by inaccessible lagoons, killing buffalo and fish and were seldom seen by anyone at all. Although they could see in the distance the white steam from the railway engines standing in Mazabuka station, they might just as well have been living on the moon.

Behind us, to the south-east, the country rose through thin bush to bare, rolling downland and then plunged almost vertically down, two thousand feet or more, to the arid, scorching valley of the Zambezi. Here lived a people almost as primitive as the Batwa but beautiful. The young girls used to polish their copper-coloured skins with castor oil and dress in little aprons of coloured beads, and they put small pink combs in their black, crinkly hair. I found several families of these people living in caves hidden in a cleft in the escarpment, and eating only roots. They said they were too frightened to build a village down in the valley or to clear any land for crops. 'The Matabele', they explained, 'used to cross the Zambezi and attack us. Supposing they came again?' If they did later summon up enough courage to defy these ancient memories, I am afraid they only had to move again because that part of the valley now lies under the waters of Lake Kariba and all the villages had to be shifted back towards the hills.

I sat one day, very hot and tired, on a sandbank by the river, not far from where the huge dam now stands. I was quenching my thirst with a water-melon and watching a large crocodile having his teeth picked by a small, white bird, when I heard a drone and looked up to see an Imperial Airways plane flying high and shining silver in the pale-blue sky. It was, I suppose, one of the first regular flights from London to Johannesburg. The intrusion of the twentieth century into this peaceful wilderness where time had never moved was startling enough. I am glad I was not there, twenty years later, to see the bulldozers come roaring in.

On that same evening, too, I saw another marvel, the undoubted spoor of an ape in the dust, like a little hand. The local villagers excitedly described not one but two big black monkeys with naked chests and I heard them bark, deeply, in the hills, but I had walked and climbed for twenty miles in great heat and I was too tired to go and look for them. I have always regretted this because there are not supposed to be any true apes in southern Africa and I allowed the only evidence of one to escape me. Perhaps the apes stayed on to breed and perhaps some Italian labourer on the dam shot one of their grandchildren, but if he did, no one ever heard of it.

Most of my time at Mazabuka, however, was spent up on the plateau where the Batonga lived with their cattle and grew large crops of maize for sale. They were prosperous people and since there were a number of mission stations in the District, they were well served with schools and with hospitals, of sorts. Their chief lack was water and this became one of our preoccupations. The men needed dams for watering their cattle and the women needed village wells at which they could draw pure water instead of having to carry it from muddy waterholes two or three miles away. It was quite easy to make these small earth dams. All the equipment needed was some iron scoops which could be pulled by oxen, to scrape up the earth and pile it on to the dam wall, like little bulldozers, and some hoes for breaking up the soil for the scoops to gather. There was no money of course — there never was — but we managed to beg some old scoops from the Public Works Department and we made several dams, some of which, after the first rainy season, held back quite sizeable little lakes. Others vanished downstream in the first spate. It was not always easy for amateurs like ourselves to choose the best sites for the dams nor, in the dry season when the stream-beds were empty, to gauge the strength and volume of the floods which the first storm would bring roaring down from the distant hills.

Wells were even more difficult to site and our methods caused much derision in technical circles. We formed a four-man African team, consisting of one water-diviner, equipped with a forked stick, one man who had worked in the mines and was qualified to use explosives and two strong labourers to dig. The villagers approved highly of the water-diviner and when his magic twig dipped they all began furiously to help with the digging. Sometimes the team found water and their percentage of dry wells was probably no greater than that of any oil-prospecting company with all its millions and all its scientific apparatus. But then it was usually not too difficult to judge from the trees and the soil whether the water-table was likely to be reasonably near the surface and sometimes the diviner's twig strained so sharply downward that he could hardly hold it. Once, when I saw this happen, I took the twig from him and marvelled how strongly it bore down on my fingers and my wrists.

A secondary purpose of these waterworks of ours was to try to persuade the Africans to copy them for themselves. At this time the policy of Indirect Rule was being introduced, which involved the formal recognition of the Chiefs' courts and also gave the tribal councils executive authority and responsibility. The courts presented no great difficulty because we had always allowed the Chiefs and their Elders to settle disputes and all that was needed now was formally to give them criminal jurisdiction and equip them with court clerks and simple records. Our part was to inspect these records as often as we could and to hear any appeals from their decisions, but these appeals were rare because all over Africa Chiefs had always been guardians of tribal law and custom and their judgments were usually acceptable to their people and nearly always to ourselves. The only difficulties we had were when African and British law conflicted. African law was supposed to prevail as between Africans when it was 'not repugnant to equity and justice', and only Africans were involved. But 'repugnant' to whom? To the people? To the District Commissioner? To the High Court?

If a villager stole a cow from his neighbour — and they often did — and he was taken before the Chief's court, it would be treated as a civil case and he would be ordered to pay back to the owner not one cow, but two. To us, as District Officers, this seemed very sensible. If, on the other hand, the owner reported his loss to the police, the culprit would be arrested and charged with the offence of stock theft before one of us sitting as a magistrate. Under the penal code he would, since stock theft was far too common, be given at least six months in gaol and the owner of the stolen cow would probably not get it back, let alone another cow as well. Personally, I never quite had the courage to try a stock theft case in the magistrate's court as a civil suit for fear of throwing the police and higher judiciary into apoplexy, but I did in the end write to my Provisional Commissioner for advice. Instead of answering he transferred me back to Mumbwa where, because of the tsetse-fly, there were hardly any cattle to be stolen.

The same sort of difficulty arose over cases of adultery, which some tribes treated as a criminal offence and others merely as an easy and pleasurable way for wives to earn money for their husbands. One stern young Chief at Mumbwa had sent his own policeman off to the Copperbelt to bring back all the girls from his villages who had gone up there to ply the trade or, as he said, to be 'Whoolies'. A dozen girls were brought back and he sentenced them all to a month in my little prison. We set the Head Messenger's wife to guard them, armed with a black umbrella, and they kept the garden weeded. Another Chief, however, who had done the same thing — because he mistakenly thought it would please the Government and not from any moral conviction — had dealt with his 'Whoolies' rather differently. He had fined them all, and those who could not pay their fine he had sent back to the mines 'to earn the money for the Government'. But then his people had the generous custom of lending their wives, for a consideration, to all and sundry.

On the whole, the tribal courts gave good justice and the less we interfered, with the different but not always superior logic of our own code of laws, the better it was for all concerned. Training those same Chiefs and Elders to executive authority, however, was very much more difficult because neither they nor their forefathers had ever exercised positive, creative authority before. They had been high priests, leaders in war and guardians of custom in a completely static society. Social and economic improvements were never imposed or even encouraged by authority. They would have been regarded as dangerous innovations certain to make the ancestors angry. Now the new authorities were expected to make bylaws and see that they were obeyed. So long as the bylaws followed established custom all was well, but no Chief could have enforced rules about keeping villages clean or not drinking too much beer, let alone making dams and wells, or he would have been deposed by public acclamation as a dangerous radical. The Batonga people were conservative.

These and similar problems of African law and a never-ending series of other cases to be tried under British law in the magistrate's court took up most of our time at Mazabuka. In the intervals, too, there were meetings of the Town Council to be attended, liaison to be maintained with the heads of the locally based departments, and all the affairs of a large European community to be attended to. It was difficult to escape from it all and to go out on *ulendo* into the villages where we were needed so much more, and we were very glad when, in 1934, we were sent once more to the familiar peace of Mumbwa.

CHAPTER 6

District Commissioner: Mumbwa

MY wife and I will never forget that journey. We decided to take two days' leave and visit some missionary friends at a place called Ibwemunyama (the 'Rock of the Animals') on top of the Zambezi escarpment. We travelled in a car which I had recently bought from the man who had made it. He had put a Morris engine on to a Ford chassis, fitted Dodge wings and wheels and built a home-made box-body of stout timber, sheathed on the outside with aluminium sheets painted bright red. To crown it all he had made an elegant wooden roof and hung it with green canvas curtains. This unique vehicle was known as 'the Scarlet Woman' and she only had one fault. Any marriage of three kinds of car would have caused consternation in Detroit and Cowley, from which they came, and they became in fact a horrid 'eternal triangle'. We discovered this when, twenty miles from Ibwemunyama and thirty miles from the nearest other settlement in totally uninhabited country, on a track with an average traffic density of one car per month, a back wheel fell off. The half-shaft had sheered through next to the hub because, presumably, Ford axles do not like Dodge wheels.

As I sat there with my wife, two very small children (our second son had arrived some months earlier), and two African servants, helpless and miles from anywhere, I touched the bottom of a motorist's despair. I looked up at a pair of eagles floating high in the pale blue sky over the tawny hills and listened to the silence. Crickets were shrilling in the heat and a dove was cooing somewhere down in the dry valley below us, but I heard no dogs barking, no cocks crowing, and no friendly clop of a woodcutter's axe. There were no villages in that waterless, stony wilderness. There were no people for miles and miles and miles.

Then a miracle happened. A truck came by. It carried us all the way to Lusaka, but I did not get the Scarlet Woman back for two months and the bill came to more than I had paid for the car itself. During the next year she dropped a wheel on two other occasions, once mercifully near home, but once when I was a hundred miles out in the bush. Eventually I sold her to a man for a very small sum and when she played the same joke on him he wisely abandoned her in the ditch into which she had tumbled him. But we loved her. She had no other vices at all, her engine ran as sweetly as a sewing-machine, and she was so light that two of us could lift her up when her back wheels sank in the mud. She also seemed to us to be the prettiest and gayest car in the whole of Central Africa.

Mumbwa is a large and empty District comprising all the tsetse-ridden country lying within the Hook of the Kafue. It is the bite of the tsetse-fly which carries sleeping sickness (in those days fatal to human beings), and kills all cattle. In order to survey the density of the fly an African (immunized by injection, of course) walked along the bush path with a white cloth pinned to the back of his shirt. A man with a notebook walked behind him and counted the flies which settled on the cloth. The results were later recorded on a graph as 'Density of Fly per Boy-Mile', a calculation which might nowadays well shock any sensitive computer.

The District contained two mission stations, one small gold mine, not more than 30,000 Africans and perhaps ten times that number of buffalo, antelope and lion. Most of it is now a National Park, but in our day we were allowed to shoot for the pot, since porters had to be fed. When we had been there four years earlier I had enjoyed hunting very much, as any young man would, and those early dawns and quiet evenings in the bush had not only given me a fine repertoire of stories and memories about animals and 'the ones which got away', but had also taught me a great deal about Africans. Indeed, the best way of getting to know the villagers was to go out hunting with them, the foolhardy, the nervous, those who knew their craft, and those who trod on twigs. It was on those long dark walks back to camp through the owl-haunted woods, when we were all relaxed, with the meat hung safely from a pole between two dark shoulders, that I heard all the gossip of the countryside. Then, one evening, I wounded an impala and one of those who were with me ran in to kill it with his spear. The game little beauty gored him from wrist to elbow with a last sweep of his lyre-shaped horns. I sold my rifle soon after that and never went hunting again if I could avoid it.

We were supposed to spend a year at Mumbwa this time, before our leave fell due, but we were so happy there that we stayed on for an extra six months. There was nobody else there, except at intervals a succession of three Cadets sent to us either to get or to get over their first experience of outstation life. For some reasons I could not understand, a 'dose of the Bradleys' was presumed to cure any Cadet's malaise, whether it was the result of an ill-tempered D.C. or just the frustration of a young, amateur anthropologist. Perhaps it was just because we were happy. We so loved our isolation that once, at the end of the rainy season, when no one had visited us for nearly six months and we heard a truck coming down the road, my wife and I looked up and said in one breath, 'I hope it doesn't stop.' We were thoroughly 'bush happy', like the crustiest of old-timers.

The problems of Mumbwa were much less complicated than those of Mazabuka, and to us much more interesting because they were those of trying to help Africans to better living in their own natural environment rather than to help them in their difficult adjustment to the conditions imposed by European settlement. Also, of course, on any outstation, the District Commissioner was king of all he surveyed, able to do what he liked and to try his hand at anything. He was road-maker, bridge-builder, doctor, teacher, detective, policeman, magistrate, farmer, cattle-breeder and, if necessary, undertaker. Above all, he was the friend of his people, who trusted him. At Mumbwa we tried all kinds of things, on the principle that if an experiment failed nobody would know about it anyway, and that if it succeeded it could be reported to headquarters and perhaps be found useful elsewhere. We grew hill rice along a stream and a flood came and washed it all away, together with our whole vegetable garden. Then we grew an experimental patch of cotton on higher ground and it flourished and became, we hoped, a starting point for a new industry. We built a rather attractive hospital of sun-dried bricks and thatch and that, too, flourished under the enthusiasm of our highly skilled African medical orderly. He had been trained in the Congo and called my wife 'Madame' which, she said, made her feel very grand. The secret of the hospital's success was that no one was allowed to die in it. As soon as the orderly knew that he could do no more for a patient, relations were allowed to take him home. That took the fear out of the white man's medicine and the last rites could be conducted in accordance with custom, as the patient went to join the ever-present ancestors in the spirit world.

I turned my court-house into a school, seconded my clerk to teach in it, and took my court cases in the shade of a great tree.

We made some cylindrical beehives out of bark and hung them up in trees for the wild bees to find, and so a little beeswax industry, which since it guaranteed a cash return for a minimum of labour, grew and flourished. We made dry-weather earth roads for five pounds a mile and maintained them for a fifth of that, and they were very good provided that no one was inconsiderate enough to use them in the rains.

One day our baby suddenly swelled up like a little Michelin-tyre man and ran a temperature of 106° with no doctor within a hundred miles. The Scarlet Woman was minus a wheel. My wife decided that he had been given green mangoes to chew which are full of turpentine, if their smell is anything to go by, and we knew that turpentine affects the kidneys. So she put him to rights with milk of magnesia. He had given us such a bad fright that we cleared a landing-strip for emergencies — even though, since there was no radio, someone would still have to bicycle that hundred miles to call an aeroplane. A small plane did turn up one day and I can remember that we were quite cross that the village people were not as astonished and as delighted and excited as we were. The white man's magic, like his medicines and his 'madness', was such that if St. Michael himself in all his glory had landed with wings spread, they could only have said the African equivalent of 'So what?' and turned away. The plane meant nothing to them or the fact that we were in swift communication with the outside world of which they knew little and cared less. Only our educated clerks and much travelled District Messengers were sufficiently interested to accept the pilot's offer of five shilling flips. When they descended from the sky they were mobbed and embraced and congratulated for their courage and daring. Years later we learned that on the West Coast of Africa the pidgin English for anti-aircraft fire was 'Plenty Humbug Steam Chicken for Up', which certainly puts the Boeing in its place.

Of all our small endeavours by far the most important were the little hospital and the other attempts we made to lessen the appalling amount of disease from which these remote, untutored people suffered. We found some cases of sleeping sickness along the banks of the Kafue, where the tsetse-fly was thickest, and a doctor came out and did a survey with me. His name was Humphrey Gilkes. How glad we were to see him! He had been best man at my wedding at Fort Jameson and had brought my elder son into the world, and we were very fond of him. His father had been Headmaster of Dulwich and one of his brothers was to become High Master of St. Paul's, but, alas, Humphrey himself was later to be killed in an air crash in East Africa.

Humphrey taught the orderly to give injections of the newly discovered Bayer 205 and about half the cases brought in to our hospital were arrested, perhaps cured. Then we had to persuade all the people to leave the infected area and go and live elsewhere. Luckily this most difficult of all administrative tasks fell to my successor. 'Density of Fly per Boy-Mile' was his headache.

Then, too, there were the family pit latrines. The Cadet and I had been discussing one evening our pet theory that, if every hut in a village were to have its own private pit latrine, the village would not have to move every few years and rebuild elsewhere because the surrounding bush had become so fouled and smelly. The people would find it worth while to build better and per-manent houses, perhaps of sun-dried brick. They could cease to be bush-burning, surface-scratching, soil-exhausting nomads, and their entire culture be transformed. It was a beautiful dream.

On the very next morning the neighbouring Chief, an intelli-gent and progressive young man, walked into the office.

'I shall have to move my village next year', he said. 'It smells and the huts are falling down.'

'Would you like to build your new village', I asked him, 'in such a way that you may never have to move again? You could even build yourself a brick house.'

'Come and see', I said, and we took him down to the Messengers' lines and showed him how behind each little brick house was its own tiny, round, and neatly thatched family pit latrine.

'They are very easy to make', I said. 'The men dig them and their wives do the thatching. These houses have been here in the same place since you were a baby on your mother's back.'

He shook his head, but he did not say as I expected him to, 'It is easy for the Government to do these things.' He said nothing at all and walked slowly away.

A few weeks later he came to me with his Elders and a few young men and said, 'These holes are good. My people have been to see them. We want them. Will you help us to plan our new village? We will start burning bricks for my court-house.'

So we found an airy site on a rise above a clear-flowing stream and together we pegged out the plan of a neat semi-circular village, with one latrine behind every house. The Cadet drew them a picture of an elegant court-house on a sheet of foolscap. Every man, woman and child worked on the project, including the brickmaking, a craft which some of the young men had learned on the Copperbelt. We used to go out on Sunday afternoons to encourage them, taking with us mango and pawpaw seeds from our own trees, and vegetable seeds, too, spinach and tomatoes, which would soon revert to their wild creeper state and need no cultivation.

The village was finished before the rains, at no cost to anybody, and very nice it was. True, the court-house leaned a bit, but so does the tower of Pisa, and true, only this and the Chief's own house were made of brick, but a start was a start.

Then the Chief said, 'Now I am going to make a law that all my people in all my villages shall dig themselves latrines or go to prison. We must be clean.' And the extraordinary thing was that his people did agree to this ruthless proposition and they did dig latrines for themselves and were very proud of them. We were not, I am glad to say, asked to put anyone in prison.

The Chief's spark had kindled a nice little fire, and very soon, since both his people and I boasted greatly of his achievement, word of it spread throughout the District. Latrines became a status symbol for all the tribes and within a year more than half the villages had begun to build them. I became known as the 'Bwana of the Latrines' and was rather swollen-headed about it — until I went to visit one very small, very remote village, nearly fifty miles away in the far bend of the Kafue.

These were people who had almost no contact with the outside world and never saw any other white man except an occasional missionary. Immediately I arrived they said, 'Come and see', and there, to my astonishment was the neatest row of family latrines I could ever hope to see, built of fresh-cut poles, thatched with sweet-smelling grass and immaculately clean. Much too clean. They had never been used.

'Oh no', they explained, 'we couldn't possibly use them. Supposing someone came and put "medicine" in one of the holes and all the family were bewitched?'

'Then why did you build them?'

'To please you.'

What could I do but smile and thank them? I hoped that one dark night some very brave old grandmother would creep out and risk using the family latrine rather than venture into the dark forest beyond, and so kindle one more spark. I also hope that just a few villages in the Mumbwa District still had latrines three years after I had been transferred elsewhere. My successor's passion was for roads.

My wife's passion was for the dissemination of garden seeds, fruit and vegetables to feed the children. This began after one tour in the dry weather when we found them wasted and dying of constipation after an unvaried diet of dried corn and water and no fruit or green vegetables. She was giving enemas all day long. No meat, no milk, no vegetables and no eggs. There were eggs, but not to eat. Nor could they be persuaded by precept or example. Anybody who ate eggs would become sterile. Was it not obvious?

'White people eat eggs and have one child, or two. We eat no eggs and have a baby every year.'

There was also the case of the gardener's twins. We were sitting, my wife and I, in our garden one Sunday afternoon when the garden boy, who lived with his wife in a hut at the bottom of the hill, came panting up the path. 'Mama!' he cried. 'Mama! Come quickly my wife is having a baby and she has only had a belly for six months.' So we ran to boil water and fetch cloths. Then a little later, as we were hurrying down the path, he met us again. 'She has had one baby and now she is having another!' This was serious, for this particular tribe did not like twins and if we did not arrive in time the second one would be thrown away to die. But we were in time, just. As we crept into the dark and smoky hut we saw one of the two old women who were acting as midwives take the second child from the mother and put it away on the floor in a corner. We were able to rescue both babies and the mother was soon up and about again. Each of the very premature twins weighed less than four pounds and they lived snugly tucked up in a flat, round grain basket, side by side, each in one leg of a pair of my wife's winter knickers. To me they were repulsive, all heads and no bodies. To her they were wonderful. She fed them from a fountain-pen filler on their own mother's milk and the funny little things thrived, which was sufficiently astonishing to merit praise from a visiting doctor and subsequent mention in *The Lancet*.

Then three months later, when they were looking almost human and were being breast-fed in the ordinary way, their mother caught pneumonia and gave it to them, and they all three died. That was a sad and rather horrible day because their father said he must bury the babies in the fork of a path lest their spirits, being twins and therefore evil, should come and haunt the family. We remembered our *Oedipus* — 'where three roads meet'.

Meanwhile, we had court cases, murders, rapes, suicides and wizardry to keep our hands in, as the representatives of law and order. Indeed, being their only representatives, we had to be detectives and policemen, too, and some of the cases taught us more about Africans than any amount of administration. Luckily the rapes usually turned out not to be rapes at all but lovers' quarrels. Wizardry was, among these particular people, more feared than deadly. It was the murders which taught us most.

We had a tradition in Northern Rhodesia that when an African had done something wrong and wished to confess it he often used to come and sit at the foot of the flagpole beneath the Union Jack. One day on my way to the office I saw a man sitting there on the grass, and as I came up to him he looked at me very gravely — he was quite young — and gently clapped his hands in greeting.

'What have you done?' I asked him.

'I have killed three men and the Government must hang me.'

'Come into the office and tell me', I said.

So we sat down together.

'I killed these three men, who were brothers, because they had all raped my sister. That is all.'

'How did you kill them?'

'I dug up some roots and squeezed the poison out of them, and I put the poison in their food. It was not a good way of killing', he added, 'but they were all strong men and I could not fight them.'

'The men had done your sister great injury and you were very angry with them, but you know as well as I do that you should have reported them to your Chief or to me and that the Government would send them to prison.'

'Yes, I knew.'

'Then why did you do this wicked thing and kill them yourself?'

'I had to. Now the Government must kill me.'

'Why did you *have* to kill?'

But he would not answer and rose and asked the Head Messenger to take him to the prison.

It would have been so easy to have verified his story and held a very short enquiry and sent him down country to be tried by the High Court on the simple facts, but I was worried. Why did he say, 'I *had* to'?

So I kept him on the station for some weeks and talked with him many times and at last he opened his heart to me.

'You see', he said, 'if I had not killed those men, the spirits of my fathers and uncles who live in the tree-tops near our village would have brought death on me and my wife and all my children, because I should have betrayed the honour of our house.'

So this young man had to fulfil his spiritual duty and, since death was inevitable in any case, he would die a happy man, and leave his family not only alive but safe. That was how his tribe had taught him to think. I had my first answer. But what about the man himself? What kind of a person was he?

When he talked to me he looked steadily into my eyes, and I liked him. I had already learned that the murderers among these people were often men of otherwise blameless character who had been driven to kill by tribal custom or religion as a spiritual duty. They were not criminals as were the thieves or those who killed for gain or those who employed witch-doctors to bring evil on their neighbours.

This was a bad case, a triple poisoning, but the young man seemed to me to be innocent of heart, and honest and certainly brave. If I had been he, I should have been faced with the same terrible alternatives of death by the rope or by the vengeance of the spirits.

Now I had to make others understand this, too, so I took a great deal of evidence from the tribal Elders to confirm all that the man had said and sent him down for trial with my blessing. In the end a merciful and experienced Governor commuted the death-sentence which the law demanded to one of not very long imprisonment, and after a few years the man, still quite young, returned to his family and, I hope, lived happily ever after.

It is, of course, pleasant to be able to recall from so many memories of this kind one at least which tells a success story to illustrate some of the lessons one learned over the years, but there were more failures than successes.

Often, indeed, I failed completely to find the truth in the tangled human situations which lay behind such crimes. I once spent a month taking evidence from twenty villagers about the murder of a stranger in their village. I felt that they were all lying and my African staff thought so too, but none of us could shake them, and in the end I sent a man whom they all accused away for trial. When the case came up in the High Court the chief witness for the prosecution suddenly cried: 'I am tired of telling lies. The man in the dock did not kill this stranger. I did.' Sensation, and many red faces, starting with mine and ending with that of the Attorney-General, who had also studied the case. A headline in the press called it 'Gilbertian Justice'.

This account of how we spent our time at Mumbwa gives a very different picture of colonial administration from that which I tried to outline in describing our first experiences at Fort Jameson eight years earlier. The administration itself had changed and already the creative ideas brought out from the Oxford and Cambridge courses by the younger, more highly trained men were beginning to influence us.

Up in Tanganyika, Bruce Hutt, a South African Rhodes Scholar and a contemporary of mine at Univ, had already published *Anthropology in Action*, as a bridge between the pure theory of men like Fraser and Malinowski and the working District Officer on the spot. Africanists like Margery Perham and Audrey Richards were already in the field being scolded and patronized by old-timers like us. In fact we gained much from their wider study and were able to put it to some practical use. But there was still no money, and because we had to make bricks without straw, we had to be content with very modest plans. The cashbook, too, had still to be balanced, and language and law examinations to be passed, and still we had to learn to be road-builders and detectives and farmers. So the young men pulled us forward and we held the reins, not, one hopes, too tightly.

CHAPTER 7

Unhappy Bureaucrat

BETWEEN 1930 and 1938 I had two spells of about two years each in the Secretariat at headquarters, the first in the old capital at Livingstone and the second at Lusaka, the new capital which was built between 1933 and 1936.

Every British dependency, at the stage when parliamentary government was in its infancy and Ministers did not yet exist, had its Secretariat. Spelt with or without the final 'e', the word has a pleasantly antique flavour of wigs and snuff, quill-pens and copperplate. Indeed, it has an honourable and ancient ancestry going back far beyond the eighteenth century. They do say that, like many English institutions, the Secretariat was a Norman invention brought to a high degree of efficiency by Henry II when the Plantagenet empire stretched from the Cheviots to the Pyrenees. Even Henry could not be everywhere at once. If there are those of us who regard this as the least praiseworthy of the many achievements of that much maligned man, let me hasten to add that he was also the archetype of the good District Officer. He was always on *ulendo*, and in his wake justice was not only done but was seen to be done. 'Where is the King?' and 'Christ! We'll have no naked men!', words given to Henry in Christopher Fry's play *Curtmantle*, would have served us for a motto. A Secretariat was, in fact, the King's Office, charged with carrying on and co-ordinating the country's administration *in Coronae absentia*, as well as of advising the King on policy. It continued in various forms and under different names right down through the centuries until ministerial government was evolved under Walpole in the eighteenth century. The rump of it survives today in the Cabinet Office.

It is not therefore so very surprising that a similar system was introduced in the British Empire when, in the early days, conditions were not all that unlike those of the Plantaganet empire in the twelfth century, and that it, too, survived until Ministries were created and the work of the Secretariats could be decentralised.

In Northern Rhodesia, as in any other dependency, the Governor was the King's representative, his Chancellor was the Chief Secretary to the Government[1] and the Secretariat was the Governor's office, presided over by the Chief Secretary, who was both executive head of the Civil Service and chief adviser to the Governor. The technical Departments, such as those of Health, Education and Agriculture, were administered by their own Directors. Policy, however, was decided by and power was ultimately centred in the Governor and his Executive Council (an embryo Cabinet), of which the Chief Secretary and the senior Heads of Departments were members. The Administration, to which the District Officers belonged, was not a Department, for we represented the Governor in our Districts and were responsible to him through the Chief Secretary.

The Secretariat, therefore, was, as it were, the nerve centre of the whole Government, through which all questions of policy passed, upwards to the Governor and the Executive Council and onwards in some cases to the Colonial Office; outwards, in the form of decisions, to Heads of Departments, and downwards, in the form of orders, to the Administration. It was also responsible for parliamentary business in the legislature, which, even in the days when the majority of the members were still officials, was always conducted like a miniature House of Commons.

With all this to do, it is not surprising that Secretariats were very busy places. Because they were concerned with every conceivable kind of problem, they were usually staffed (except for one or two specialists), not by technicians, but by District Officers, who were supposed to be able to turn their hands to anything. The practice was to select promising young men from the Administration and to bring them into the Secretariat for a while, both to widen their horizons and to test their capacity. If they had

[1] This was his title in a Protectorate. In a Crown Colony he was called the Colonial Secretary.

a flair for the work they might well stay in the Secretariat or be brought back into it after more experience in the Districts, and end up, perhaps, as Chief Secretaries or even Governors. If they turned out to be more suited for administration in the field than on files they went back to their Districts and might end as Provincial Commissioners[1] or even, occasionally, as Governors of small and uncomplicated colonies. It was a good system, both from the point of view of the men themselves, who were given an opportunity to discover their own talents and shortcomings, and from that of the Governments, because it built up efficient Secretariats staffed, in their senior posts, by some of the most able men in the Administration.

It suited the Colonial Office too because it was able to recruit experienced men from the Secretariats to the highest posts in other dependencies with some certainty that they were the best available. The chief drawback of the system was that the young District Officers in the lower reaches of the Secretariat were always changing and always inexperienced, which was a trial both to their superiors and to the Heads of Departments who had to deal with them. So much so, indeed, that, as time went on and Secretariats grew ever larger with the increasing quantity of work resulting from economic and social development, a tendency arose to keep the most suitable of the young men in the Secretariat. This unfortunately deprived them of the further experience in the field which they needed if they were, in later years, to avoid becoming too remote and bureaucratic in their outlook, but it was probably inevitable.

There was always a lot of criticism of the Secretariat, and of the people in it, both among District Officers and the departmental staffs, just as there is always criticism of the 'brass hats' in the army among regimental officers and, I suppose, of any headquarters organization of any kind. It is inevitable because of the difficulty of communication between those on the ground who often cannot see the wood for the trees down among which they work, and

---

[1] Northern Rhodesia was divided up into eight Provinces, each in charge of a Provincial Commissioner and each containing several Districts in charge of District Commissioners, who were responsible to him.

those on the heights above who cannot see the trees for the wood. If a man is trying to build a road and wants another £100 in order to complete it, he cannot be expected to appreciate that there are a dozen other men who are also demanding £100 to finish other jobs which to them are equally important. If there is not enough money to go round, he will dislike being told to leave his road unfinished until the next budget produces some more. Nor is it easy for the man in the Secretariat to judge such priorities correctly, let alone to understand how very important one small bush-road may seem to the lonely District Officer who thought of it, and started it, and does so want to finish it before he goes on leave.

Yet, the odd thing was that almost every one of those highly critical District Officers who were so scornful of 'jumped-up Secretariat types', 'soulless bureaucrats' and 'careerists', was secretly delighted if he were offered a Secretariat posting. Off he would go to headquarters, grumbling, apprehensive, but inwardly aglow with new-kindled ambitions, for the Secretariat was, they said, the ladder to fame and glory. We were, after all, as Falstaff said to his Prince, 'Mortal men, my Lord, mortal men.'

That, at any rate, was how I felt when I was sent for from Mkushi in 1928. The fact that I was the only man who had as yet been seconded to the Colonial Office and might therefore be presumed to have learnt the elements of drafting letters and despatches and writing minutes in files, or that the Secretariat, with the opening up of the Copperbelt, was desperately under-staffed and was therefore scraping the barrel for talent, did not, I suspect, enter my head.

In those days the Secretariat in Livingstone was very small, with an executive staff of less than ten and perhaps twenty clerks. It was housed in a ramshackle row of tin-roofed wooden offices at the back of Government House, which was also ramshackle and made of wood.

I found myself in charge of a section, staffed by two highly efficient European girls, Susan and Edith, and one African clerk. We were responsible for about a thousand files. Some of these dealt with agriculture, others with education and police matters, but a growing number carried that label 'Miscellaneous' which seems to be inevitable in any filing system and is always guaranteed to grow larger, more amorphous and more disastrously confusing. Every letter which came into the Secretariat and had no obvious home in any other section ended up in my MISC series. It housed within its yellow files every kind of problem from complaints about the postal service to extradition proceedings.

MISC included, I remember, the case of an American who had been engaged by our Public Works Department and now turned out to be wanted in the States for murder. After his arrest he escaped from the Livingstone gaol by the time-honoured means of filing through the bars, bluffed his way past the South African frontier at Mafeking, although the police should have had his photograph on the table in front of them, and was finally picked up by them when he was boarding a ship for India at Durban. He had guileless blue eyes and a most engaging charm and he had everybody fooled.

My work was hard, harassing and endless, but it was not very responsible. Susan looked after the files and put them up to me in impeccable order. I put them up in my turn to the next level in our little pyramid of power, sometimes with comments and suggestions, which were usually valueless, and after a few days down they would come again with instructions to write letters, draft despatches to the Colonial Office, or to find that bugbear of bureaucracy a 'precedent'. Edith did the shorthand and typing, and once I had overcome that paralysis of mind and voice which attacks everyone the first time he is confronted by a pretty stenographer with pencil poised, I quite enjoyed doing the correspondence. It was fun to sit at the bottom of the pyramid and to see how good minds worked and how policy was made.

Because the Secretariat was so small, and because the Chief Secretary was a brilliant man with a fine, incisive mind, and because his principal assistant was imaginative and kind, the office was happy and, by government standards, efficient (most letters being answered within a couple of weeks or so), and we youngsters got a very good training.

The only trouble was that there was far too much work. All of us took files home every night and worked on both Saturday and Sunday mornings, trying to keep abreast of the problems of a rapidly developing economy.

A time came when every executive officer in the Secretariat except the Chief Secretary and myself was either in hospital from overwork or taking short leave under doctor's orders. For two memorable weeks we two were alone and I remember them, not because the ship of state flooded and foundered, but because it never, before or since, moved more swiftly or more smoothly. I collected the mail in the morning and took it to him. He read it and divided the letters into two piles, easy and difficult. He told me what to do on the easy ones, he kept the others, and we both dictated to the girls. Then, in the evening, we signed all the letters. All over the country people were amazed to get answers out of the Secretariat by return of post, for such a thing had certainly never happened before. This was due partly to the brilliance of the Chief Secretary, whose mind worked with awe-inspiring speed and clarity, and partly to the fact that there were only two of us so that no time was spent on collecting precedents, minuting on files, or drafting letters for approval. It was an exhilarating experience while it lasted, but of course it could not have continued for long. All the more important and compli-cated matters of policy had to be put into cold storage until somebody had the time to *think* about them. Never were IN and OUT trays emptied or PENDING trays filled more quickly.

If life in Livingstone was hard, it was also merry. We lived in a dreadful little house and were very poor. We were definitely living above our station, and my wife took a job in the local school to help pay the bills. Every evening I had my head down among the yellow files until I could no longer keep awake. But between four and six in the afternoons and at weekends we lived, revelling in all the delights of civilization which our outstations could not give us: golf and tennis, the cinema, dances at the Club, cocktail parties, and meeting lots and lots of new people, including distinguished visitors from the outside world. One of them, I remember, was General Smuts. Livingstone was small enough to be friendly and it suffered little from that curse of most colonial capitals, official snobbery.

Best of all was the river, the wide, blue, beautiful Zambezi, and the glory of the Victoria Falls. On Sundays we would take picnics to the palm-crowned islands or stalk crocodiles in the reed-beds, or go scrambling in the seventy miles of zigzag gorges below the Falls. When the river was low we could pick our way over rocks out into midstream, just above the Falls, to bathe in a deep pool known to us as the 'Armchair' which hung on the very lip of the abyss. We could lie flat with our toes in the pool behind us and our chins hanging over 400 feet of nothing.

Yet, whenever business took me to the office of the local District Commissioner and I saw the quiet groups of African villagers sitting under the trees awaiting their turn to talk to him, my heart turned over. There was a real Africa out there beyond the files and the telephone wires and I must get back to it.

So I did, for four blissful years, before I was once more called in to take over the same old section in a much bigger Secretariat in the brand-new capital at Lusaka. But now the Secretariat was not the same. It had grown from a compact little team into a real bureaucracy. The Copperbelt had grown very quickly in the intervening years and now consisted of a series of great industrial centres, each with its new and splendidly equipped attendant township, the whole forming a concentration of highly developed 'civilization' surrounded by thousands of square miles of emptiness.

From this growth the Government was getting more revenue but also many more problems. At the same time, Britain's colonial policy had begun to move in a more positive and constructive way and the Colonial Service itself was beginning to move from the age of the amateur into that of the specialist.

The great economic depression of the early thirties had only halted development for a few short, anxious months, giving the Government time to get its breath and to set its machinery in order. Then things began to move again and a second cycle of expansion started.

'Parkinson's Law' began to operate and the Secretariat grew

and grew. There was no chance now of the Chief Secretary and one junior officer running it together in an emergency. The Chief Secretary was now a remote and august person whom one very rarely saw. All one did see, really, were floods of files flowing to and fro with little apparent urgency, punctuated by crises, accompanied, usually on Saturday mornings, by frantic flurries of telegrams and shrilling, insistent telephones.

I did not like any of this. Some 'organization man', for instance (a species to be carefully distinguished from the administrator, for the one thinks only in terms of machinery and files and the other in terms of people), had taken all the highly efficient little file registries away from the sections and collected them all together in one big central registry, from which letters took days to emerge and where urgently wanted papers often could not be found. From forty years' experience I have formed only two conclusions about filing systems: never try to reform them or you will make confusion worse confounded, and never have a central registry. Where missing papers are concerned there is, in the last desperate search, no substitute for the human memory and if you leave the files in the personal care of those who have to use them, they will guard them like their children and keep them clean, tidy and in order.

I now spent my days trying to be intelligent about problems which I did not understand because they lay outside my own experience, such as schemes for scientific research, and such educational mysteries as 'middle' and 'normal' schools. After a while, however, I was given an opportunity to act in a more senior post, while the occupant was on leave, and found myself to my joy concerned entirely with African affairs. I was back among Chiefs and African councils and the familiar grumbles and enthusiasms of District Officers, which I did understand and where I really could help.

Chiefly I was concerned to try to establish closer and more friendly contact between the Secretariat and the District Officers in the field, and here I was very fortunate because the man for whom I worked during those few months was an intensely human and dynamic person. Eric Dutton had a great zest for living and, among other violent prejudices, a contempt for red tape and all that it stood for. Lamed from the First World War and usually in pain, he was understandably bad-tempered and difficult, but he had a deep understanding of, and sympathy with, people and, almost as important, he had an intensely creative and positive imagination. He and I went on tour together, doing a lot of business on the Copperbelt and in other busy places as well as remote outstations, and everywhere he went he had private talks with the District Officers and, I think, made friends with them. I remember how surprised and pleased he was that, although they all asked for money for their own pet schemes, nobody asked for anything for himself. All of this was useful and exciting and fun, but, alas, my 'acting' period was all too short and in 1938 I found myself again down among those familiar yellow files, and all their still unfamiliar subjects.

Very soon after this I was sent for and told, reproachfully, that I was too 'young-minded'. I have been puzzling about this ever since. If they meant that I was naïve and optimistic, I can only say that thirty years later, I still am. What they meant was, perhaps, that my critical faculty was weak and that I was not sensitive enough to other people's reactions and therefore had shown very little political ability in my dealings either with other officials or with the members of the now much more important Legislative Council. These very real weaknesses added up to the inescapable fact that, in spite of all my experience, I was not the 'Secretariat type' and would never be a good Chief Secretary.

I did not understand this at the time and they were, perhaps, too kind to explain it to me. Therefore, it came as a considerable shock to be told, a few weeks later, that I must leave the Secretariat and return to a District, even though they did soften the blow by telling me that I could return to Fort Jameson as District Commissioner.

The truth of the matter is, I suppose, that bureaucracies need men with detached, critical and well-balanced minds who can weigh up problems and see what is wrong and what is right in other people's proposals, and give considered judgments. That is what bureaucrats are for, and these were the men who, in the

Colonial Service, became Chief Secretaries. Others, who were too critical and had insufficient sympathy and imagination, became the ossified 'soulless bureaucrats' so often and so wrongly taken as typical of the whole breed. Those who had too much creative imagination and were better at doing things than thinking about them would never make good Chief Secretaries, though they might well make good Governors. Occasionally men rose up through the Secretariat who combined all these qualities of detachment, criticism, imagination and decisiveness, and these made the finest Governors of all.

One of the traps which lay in wait for all alike was, inevitably, ambition, and that alone was many a man's undoing, for there should be little room for self-seeking in the public service. An element of ambition was there, of course, in all of us, because, as I have said, the Secretariat was the ladder to higher things, but there are two kinds of ambition. The one makes you try to do your job well for its own sake and in the hope that merit may be recognized; the other makes you thrust yourself up the ladder, kicking anybody off it who blocks your way or looks like competing with you. I have known men like this who climbed quite high (and I hope they enjoyed it), but only one or two of them in the Colonial Service ever got to the top.

We had enjoyed the life in Lusaka. The site chosen for the new capital was a long low bush-covered ridge, rising from a flat plateau about two miles east of the existing town on the railway line. The plateau country was not beautiful, but at over 4,000 feet above the sea it had, by African standards, a splendid, invigorating climate. After the steamy heat of Livingstone this was something to be prized. The new town had been carefully planned on a spacious scale by experts from England as the nucleus of a future city. Already it was a more attractive place than anyone could have expected it to be. This was largely due to the imagination and drive of Eric Dutton. He took a deep personal interest in the whole project and harried the town-planners and architects to distraction. He also made it his business to beautify the whole place with trees and flowering shrubs. He collected seeds and seedlings from all over the tropical world, and grew them in a nursery round which he stumped, and swore and rejoiced. Then he planted them himself not only along all the roads but in the gardens of all the Government houses. He was a ruthless enthusiast and a demon of energy.

We found ourselves living in a brand-new, double-storeyed house with a large garden and we asked for oleander, frangipani and other exotic shrubs to put in it. 'Right!' said Dutton. 'Dig ten square holes, three-by-three-by-three — feet, not inches.' When we were ready he came with a lorry and two Africans. In went the shrubs and they flourished in great beauty. But woe betide those who had dug their holes round instead of square or two by two by two. One look, one blast of scorn, and away he would go in his corduroy trousers, yellow shirt and red scarf, stumping along on the stick which his war-wound compelled him to use. His lorry with the precious shrubs still on board would roar away in a cloud of red dust and the digging had to be done again.

Even in 1936 one road was glorious with a double avenue of blue jacaranda, shimmering softly in the October heat. The mile-long Ridgeway had already been planted with little wild fig trees that would one day be giants casting deep, cool shade.

When I visited Lusaka in 1964 I was delighted to find how faithfully the main outlines drawn by the town-planners thirty years before had been followed. Lusaka is now a city, complete with mayor and corporation, but it is still so spacious and so rich in trees and lawns and brilliant gardens that it looks much more like a garden suburb than a city.

The new buildings which have been put up since the war include not only office blocks, flats and houses, but also several schools and colleges and a cathedral. They are, of course, contemporary in design, but they do not conflict with the neo-classical style in red brick and tile of those built in the thirties because all the buildings are widely spaced and there are so many trees to isolate them one from another. The avenues of blue jacaranda, yellow acacias and scarlet flame-of-the-forest trees, planted in those early days, are now twenty to thirty feet tall, just as we once imagined them when they were only seedlings.

All the other trees and shrubs which we planted in our gardens

G

are now so tall and thick that I had great difficulty in finding the house in which we once lived. My fearsome friend in his corduroy trousers and red neckerchief would be delighted if he could go back and see it all. In particular, perhaps, he would be glad to know that his mile-long column of African fig trees all along Ridgeway is there and is flourishing though, being wild and slow of growth, they are not yet giants. It was, indeed, a pleasant and all-too-rare experience to return to find a dream come true. Usually to return to a place where one has been young and happy is unrewarding. Memory will have left a picture of false loveliness in the mind and the reality is disappointing.

Yet I do remember that when the time came for me to leave Lusaka in 1938 I was glad to go. I had come to accept my sentence of exile and the seeming end to a Secretariat career with relief and no real disgruntlement. My wife went home to Oxford, where my elder son was already at the Dragon School, to which the younger must now go. I loaded up a lorry with all our packing-cases and our Ford Prefect with the servants and Paddy, the wire-haired terrier, and set off for Fort Jameson, along the 300 miles of potholes, euphemistically called the Great East Road. It was good to have a road of any kind. At least I would not have to travel to Fort Jameson via Johannesburg as I had done twelve years before. With every mile of potholes my spirits rose.

That evening, as we bumped our way down through furnace heat into the deep Luangwa Gorge and I could see beyond it the escarpment which guarded my old and most favourite stamping ground, the trumpets sounded for me and I sang to the echoing hills.

CHAPTER 8

Return to Fort Jameson

FORT JAMESON had changed little between 1926 and 1938. The tobacco industry had only partially recovered from the depression which had intervened and the number of planters had dwindled. The African population, however, had been growing quickly, as it had done in all our colonies ever since the *Pax Britannica* began. The overcrowding in the African Reserves had been added to by a steady influx of Achewa from Portuguese territory.

To lack of employment and a growing scarcity of land in the African Reserves was added shortage of administrative staff. Whereas in 1926 Cartmel Robinson, as D.C., had had three and sometimes four District Officers and Cadets to help him, I now had one Cadet and, for a very short time, one District Officer seconded as Labour Officer, who was concerned only with the planters and their employees. The only signs of progress were an agricultural research station some miles from the town and the addition to the technical staff in the District of an Education Officer to supervise the very large number of mission schools. There was also one small mechanical grader, which helped to smooth out the corrugations in the roads. Blackwater fever, which in the old days had killed one or two European planters each rainy season, had been overcome. Blackwater is blood in the urine due to chronic neglected malaria. But malaria was still very much with us.

Fort Jameson had remained a happy and friendly sort of place. Ox-waggons still stood in its wide, tree-shaded roads. Slouch-hatted planters still crowded the club bar on Saturday mornings. We were still protected from the outside world by 300 miles of dusty road, and by the enfolding hills.

The D.C.'s house, up under the hill beyond the golf course, was very big, and the Cadet agreed to share it with me. We became very good friends and lived harmoniously, the more so, perhaps, because we were seldom at home together for more than a week at a time. Each of us spent three weeks in the month out on *ulendo* trying, since close administration is good administration, to visit every one of our 1,100 villages each year. This meant very long hours and very hard work both for the man on the station and for the man on *ulendo*. Nor was there much rest when we were together. It was not, however, the work which, now and then, brought us low. It was malaria. Yellow pills would keep it at bay when we were fit, but they failed when we were tired and our resistance low. Only when each of us had been ignominiously brought in semi-conscious from *ulendo* by an indignant doctor did we slow the programme down a little.

With constant touring such a big District could just be managed by two people and, when the Labour Officer left, the planters helped us by not bringing their troubles to the office, but waiting for us to call on them at their homes when we were visiting near-by villages. They much preferred to talk over their problems with us on their own verandas and in their own tobacco fields, where they were at home and confident. We, for our part, found them, as hosts who appreciated our coming to them, much more amenable than they were as visitors to our unattractive offices, who had made a hot, dusty and inconvenient journey to reach us. Our only trouble was that we had to drink so many cups of tea. They seemed to live on it. With one or two exceptions they were reasonable people and they responded well to this peripatetic type of administration, as, indeed, did the Africans for very much the same reasons.

There were, however, exceptions. One whom I vividly re-member was a man of great strength and uncertain temper. One day, just as I was packing up to go on *ulendo*, this man had a quarrel with a neighbouring farmer and knocked him out. The police reported this and I sent for him.

'You', I said, 'are being a nuisance. I'm just leaving and I'm not going to cancel my trip merely to try you for assault. Will you promise me to stay on your farm and behave yourself till I come back?'

'Of course', he said.

That evening the Inspector of Police came to me and said: 'I hear that this man swears he is coming into town on Saturday evening to beat up the hotel.'

'Why? He has promised not to come in.'

The policeman gave me a pitying look. 'He will', he said, 'because the other fellow will be there.'

'So', I said, 'that cheers up your Saturday evening too, because you will have to sit in the bar there all the evening, to stop any trouble.'

When I came back three weeks later, I found the vast and formidable man sitting in my office, scowling.

'Do I understand', he said, 'that you put a policeman in the hotel the other Saturday in case I turned up?'

'Just a precaution', I replied cautiously.

'But I gave you my word. I haven't put a foot off my farm, and not had one drink in three weeks. Do you think I'd let you down? If so, come on outside and we'll settle it properly.'

'Who, me?' I said. I am a very small man.

Then he roared with laughter and we went off and had a drink together. Next day he paid a handsome fine for assaulting his friend and that was the end of that.

For the most part, however, we were concerned about the Africans. The land shortage in the Reserves had become so acute that the people did not have enough to eat. The trouble was that long ago a commercial company had bought a concession from a German which he had obtained from the Paramount Chief of the Angoni. By virtue, if that is the word, of this concession they now owned ten thousand square miles of land, much of which they could neither sell nor develop, and on which the Africans were not allowed to live. The Africans called them 'the silent lands'. It was only too clear to us, as we travelled through the Reserves in the over-cultivated and eroded hills and on the crowded, dusty plateau that the problem must be tackled in three ways. First, more water must be supplied in those parts of the Reserves which could not be lived in for lack of it. Second, African farming methods must be improved to halt erosion and to increase production. Thirdly, we must persuade the Government to buy up all or most of the 'silent lands' for African occupation. It would cost a frightening amount.

For a year we softened up the defences of headquarters by a continuous bombardment of reports describing the disgraceful conditions in the various Reserves. Then, with the help of the Agricultural Officer, we launched our main attack in the form of a report covering the whole District. It was a fat, impressive volume, gay with maps coloured from a child's paintbox and crowded with statistics. It had a cool reception because its recommendations were so costly. In the end, and just in time, the Government did, a year or two later, buy up all the 'silent lands'. So there was a happy ending after all, and the sum that was in fact paid after much negotiation was about what we had prophesied. That's negotiation, that is.

Making dams and sinking wells would no longer be left to the amateur with his water-diviner and his old man with a blasting certificate. The improvement of water supplies had now become a matter for experts. The Government had set up a special Department, professionally staffed. They asked the Head of it, a distinguished geologist, to come and look over the waterless parts of the Reserves. He and I walked together through many miles of lifeless woodlands, and after I had left the District the technicians moved in and dams and wells appeared.

In one or two places amateur wells already existed, built by some previous D.C., and I remember one of them particularly because of the lesson it taught me. When the Chief and I arrived in the village we found the well in a very sad state. It had been given a brick coping, crowned with cement, a roof, a windlass, and a big bucket on a long wire cable. It had cost quite a few pounds, no doubt 'fiddled' out of the road vote or some other irrelevant pocket of the Government. Now the cement had been broken off. Most of the bricks were gone and the cable and bucket had vanished. The people were lowering their own water-pots down into the well on knotted lengths of bark-rope. Both the ground near by and the water itself were fouled and certainly teeming with a lethal assortment of germs. The Chief said, 'Leave this to me', and sent for the villagers.

'You have', he said, 'taken the wire rope and melted it down to make spears. You have taken the cement to sharpen them. You have stolen the bucket. This was your own well, given to you by the Government. Now you will pay to have it mended by me, your Chief. Every man in the village will pay threepence and, since drawing water is woman's work, every married man will pay another threepence for each of his first two wives.'

The results were as impressive as his economy of words. They paid up to a man, the well was mended, and it was, I am sure, quite a long time before another levy was needed.

As I watched the villagers hurry to their huts to find carefully hidden threepences, I was thinking of an abortive exercise I had once tried at Mumbwa.

On the upper reaches of the Kafue not very far from the Copperbelt there lived a certain village headman who had built himself a very good house. One day he called his people together and he said to them: 'When the harvest is in, all you young men will go away to the copper mines and work, and you will take your wives with you. Then, in six months time when the little stars (the Pleiades) are in the sky and it is time to sow the maize again, you will all come back and you will stay at home until harvest-time and we shall all be here together for the other half of the year.'

Since the headman was liked and respected, so it happened, every year from then on. The result was so startling a revolution in the standard of living of his people as I am sure the headman, who had only been concerned for the preservation of his community, could not possibly have foreseen. The young men and women came home rich not only in money and new possessions, but also in new ideas about better and cleaner houses and, even more important, with the habit of regular work. Within two years they had rebuilt the whole village. Every neat, new house had a window in it and the clean white walls were decorated with designs in coloured clays. Everybody was busy working together both in the fields and in beautifying their homes and nobody quarrelled very much and they were happy.

Some miles away there lived another tribe whose villages were disgraceful. The men were lazy and their women were sluts. They lived in tumbledown huts and they were dirty, diseased and witch-ridden. Why not, I thought, show these people what the other village had done and persuade them to follow its example? So I went and told them all about it.

I ended half an hour's impassioned oratory with the announcement that on the very next morning we would all set off to see the village I had been describing. I sat down and wiped the sweat off my forehead and waited for the impulsively enthusiastic speeches which my own enthusiasm usually evoked. 'Any questions?' Not with these people. They sat and looked at the ground and then, at last, the elderly, dignified but quite ineffective Chief stood up.

'Will the Government', he asked — and I swear he was not being sarcastic — 'give me a pair of boots?'

Nobody turned up the next morning. As I walked miserably away from that smelly village through the long, dew-soaked grass and the fresh sunlit woods, I wondered what else I could have done, except talk.

I was thinking now too of something which the Agricultural Officer had told me only a few days before on his research station outside Fort Jameson. Convinced that one ocular demonstration was worth more than hours of exhortation he had grown two plots of maize. One of them had been properly manured with cow dung and carefully weeded. The other had been grown in the normal village manner with no manure and very little weeding. When the crops had ripened, the one was rich and tall and fruitful, the other stunted, with half the yield. He had shown them to a large party of local villagers, enthusiastically convinced that this practical demonstration would do more to induce them to become better farmers than all his previous sermons.

They came and saw and clicked their tongues in admiration and then they said, 'It is wonderful what the Government can do with all its money.'

'But', cried my friend, 'each crop was grown by the same four men, and each cost exactly the same amount. The only difference was that they put more work into one crop than the other.' They did not believe him and went away shaking their heads. My friend could only hope that perhaps one day just one of them would try digging a few head-loads of cattle dung into his lands.

Yet this Chief, into whose cupped hands the threepences were pouring, was getting results and that Mumbwa headman had got them, too.

Clearly, their own people could lead them. Rather, perhaps, some of them could. This, I thought, was at once the strength and the weakness of the whole system of Indirect Rule. Some of the Chiefs, Elders and village headmen were capable and progressive. Others were neither and the well-being of their people varied accordingly.

Pondering on these matters we at Fort Jameson decided to try an experiment. We persuaded several of the Chiefs' Councils among the Angoni to appoint some young educated men to the Councils and to put them in charge of various activities. One, for example, became Minister of Latrines, and another Minister of Better Houses. This idea was taken up with some enthusiasm, and resulted quite quickly in visible improvements in the villages. It was, even though elections were still too un-African to be thought of by anybody, the first step towards the development of local government on Western democratic lines. Our Governor, who was something of an amateur anthropologist, reprimanded me, and told us to find out who the traditional office-bearers of the Angoni were. We must stop introducing such alien ideas. The Chiefs, who were not anthropologists, pointed out that there never had been office-holders of this kind and, in any case, the people were interested in the future and not in the past. So they were allowed to keep their Ministers and a too anthropological and obscurantist approach to tribal administration was not allowed to stop the wheels of progress almost before they had begun to turn.

Indeed, one of the chief purposes of Indirect Rule, as we saw it, was to encourage self-help in every possible field. The real objection to colonial government, at that early stage of social development before nationalism had come to supersede tribal loyalties, was not its alien rule, but its paternalism. — 'Will the Government give me a pair of boots?' — the people expected the Government to do everything. Did it not have power, and wisdom and riches beyond imagining?

One day, quite soon after the Angoni had appointed their first young Ministers, one of the Chiefs' Councils, no doubt at the suggestion of its enthusiastic Minister for Schools, came to us in a body. There were, they said, four missionary societies working among their people and all their children were being brought up to be Roman Catholics, or Anglicans, or Calvinists or Seventh Day Adventists and to despise each other as heretics or fools. These were strong words but not perhaps too strong. Sectarianism had always been rife in the District and its social effects were wholly bad. I had myself in earlier days found notices pinned to trees by adherents to one sect saying that the teachers of another were known to be cannibals.

'To us', said the Chief, 'a man is either a Christian or he is not. What kind of Christian he is does not matter. What does matter is that our children should be brothers and grow up together as good Angoni. Will the Government give us our own school?' This was better than asking for boots, but it was still not good enough.

'Why don't you build it yourselves?' I suggested.

'No money.'

'No, but you have five thousand people each with two hands, and good earth for making bricks, and trees for poles, and any amount of thatching grass.'

They stared at me and I saw a spark kindle in the Chief's eye, and in the eye of his bright young Minister.

'Yes', said the Chief thoughtfully. 'We have some bricklayers too and some carpenters in the villages. But', quick as a flash, 'what about schoolbooks and teachers? Who pays?'

'You could levy an education rate. The people won't mind paying when they have built a fine school for themselves and are proud of it. Let's build it first and see about money afterwards.'

We persuaded the local Public Works Department man to draw us simple plans and to donate tools and nails and even some cement. We enrolled the Agricultural Officer to lay out the school gardens. Everyone in the neighbourhood set to work. The men cut the poles for the roofs, the women cleared the site and cut the long grass for the thatch. The small boys helped to tread out the mud for making bricks. The Chief and his Minister found one or two carpenters and bricklayers and raised the money to pay them. They were here, there and everywhere, exhorting, cursing, cajoling, usually followed by a flock of knee-high excited children. Great enthusiasm was generated and towards the end of the six rainless months between harvest and sowing their school was finished in a last wave of singing and a splendid beer party.

Meanwhile the Chiefs' Council had agreed to raise an education levy to pay for schoolbooks and we found for them three experienced teachers, each of whom had been discarded by a different missionary society for marrying more than one wife. Otherwise they were pillars of Christian rectitude. I had, too, raised my own levy of pencils, pens, ink-bottles, and many other necessities from all our offices. The Education Officer persuaded his Department to make a grant to pay the teachers' salaries.

We opened the school in 1938, with seventy-five pupils, some of whom were weekly boarders. They lived in rather pretty little houses and there was a quite imposing classroom block. I believe that same Ngoni school still flourishes today, though doubtless it has long since acquired more permanent and much more professional buildings. Then the Achewa built one, too, and Native Authority Schools, as they came to be called, later sprang up in other parts of the country.

This modest experiment in self-help was typical of many others which District Officers were beginning to make, often on a much larger scale, in different parts of British Africa for exactly the same reasons as ours: lack of money for the roads, dispensaries and schools which the people needed and a growing conviction that spoon feeding was a bad thing. So readily did the people respond to the idea of self-help and so quickly did the idea spread that, soon after the end of the Second World War, Community Development, Mass Literacy campaigns and agricultural co-operative and self-help schemes of all kinds became a recognized and important part of Colonial Office policy.

That it should all have happened like this was typical of the empirical approach which was always characteristic of British colonial administration. Indirect Rule itself began when Lord Lugard decided that it would be better and cheaper to allow the Emirs of newly occupied Northern Nigeria to continue to rule their peoples in the traditional manner, rather than to substitute a British bureaucracy. Thirty years later it developed into the official policy for all the African dependencies. Similarly, hundreds of small independently conceived experiments in self-help eventually came to be translated into a policy, and presently there was a whole new philosophy of administration for all under-developed countries, with its own title, its own jargon, and its own academic school of theorists. Community Development under different names has spread all over the tropical world from Latin America to Thailand. In India alone the Village Aid Development programme is bringing higher standards of living and more happiness to millions. This and all the other schemes based on the principle of self-help have probably been, in terms of human happiness, the most valuable contribution made by the West to the underdeveloped world.

At Fort Jameson the only other experiment of this kind that we had time to try was the building of two or three rural dispensaries in the remotest parts of the District. The villagers built them and the Medical Department then equipped them with dressings and drugs and dispensers sufficiently trained at least to know when a case was serious enough to be sent to hospital.

At that time there were no farmers' co-operative societies, though they were started soon afterwards in the neighbouring District, where the Africans grew tobacco. Our efforts to improve farming methods were concentrated on the introduction of rice and cotton as cash crops in the Luangwa Valley. This the Agricultural Officer saw to with great success. There was also a lot of discussion as to the best way of persuading the people in the hills to contour-ridge their maize gardens. They grew their maize in little mounds, so why not grow it on little ridges instead, piled up with hoes along the contours? It was perhaps a good idea — at least it had the essential virtue of simplicity — but it remained only an idea because we were far more concerned about trying to get new land for the people than with helping them to improve what they had.

Although it was not possible to do all that we wanted to do, because there were so few of us and because there were only seven days in the week, those eighteen months at Fort Jameson were, so far as my work was concerned, the happiest and most rewarding in all my experience as a District Officer. So much so, in fact, that when a well-intentioned Government sent round a circular asking each of us to say where we would like to be stationed, if we had a choice, and for how long, I simply replied, 'Fort Jameson, always'. The reason for this contentment was not, I am sure, power over people, which one always had as D.C. of a large and complex District, but the freedom one had to experiment on a worth-while scale with new and exciting ideas. Administration had become creative. For me, at least, creating new things in one form or another is an essential ingredient of the good life. Some people, they say, are 'creators' and others 'maintainers'. The happy man is he who discovers which he is in time to order his life accordingly. I knew by the time I was thirty-four that maintaining bored me and though life has since imposed periods of maintenance upon me at least I have usually recognized the nature of their frustrations and have been lucky enough in the end to escape from them.

At Fort Jameson too I began to learn something else of even greater importance. People, I found, were more interesting than things and I liked being involved in their lives and problems. Everything which the administrator does affects the lives of others, and in his planning and its execution he must try to put himself into the minds of his people. Human beings are not statistics or lines on a graph. It was more difficult, I discovered, to accept the involvement in other people's lives which this entailed and at the same time to retain that detachment which was just as essential. It was only too easy to abandon some project that was right in itself because one began to feel too strongly the force of other people's protests. Always there came a point when one had to stand back and look at the project again and say, sometimes,

'This is right — we will do it', and then renew the battle for their minds and hearts.

All this, of course, applied even more to one's dealings with colleagues and staff than to those with the Europeans and Africans whose business we were always so busy minding. One's colleagues had also to be one's friends and not every man has the gift of friendship. At Fort Jameson I think I must have been very fortunate.

CHAPTER 9

Learning to Write

THEY say that every man has at least one good book in him. Perhaps the *Diary of a District Officer*, which I wrote after my return to Fort Jameson, was mine.

That I should have always wanted to write was, I suppose, inevitable because so many of my family had done so.

This much in the way of a literary bent I was born with, but if in my twenties, married and poor, I had not been driven to write a story in order to pay the rent, it is only too probable that I, like so many others whose fingers only faintly itch, would never have written anything at all, but would have spent the rest of my life saying that I would do so when I had the time. Blank foolscap is so discouraging. The dog simply must be taken for a walk.

Someone long ago has said that the best and crispest writing is done with a road-drill outside, the bailiffs at the door and an editorial or theatrical deadline looming close ahead. Certainly, almost everything I have ever had published has been written under pressures of this kind and nearly always in the evenings or at weekends or on holidays, in such occasional hours as could be squeezed out of a hard-working life. I feel, too, that I am not well equipped. I left school and the university ill-read (except in Greek and Latin), prejudiced and cursed with a memory that to this day refuses to retain the written word at all and clings only to visual images.

So far as the craft of writing is concerned, I learned, it seems to me, only three useful lessons when I was young, on rhythm, compression and simplicity. I was fascinated to discover that Cicero achieved splendid rhythm by ending all his rolling sentences with a selection of closing metres which scanned like poetry. I admired the skill with which Tacitus etched into his reader's imagination with the cutting edge of ruthless economy and precise selection of words. And then there was Sir Walter Raleigh, who had been Merton Professor of English at Oxford shortly before my time. He wrote, in a book called *On Writing and Writers* — 'If you talk nonsense in Saxon you are found out at once; you have a judge in every hearer. But put it into Latin and the nonsense masquerades as profundity of abstract thought.' I have never forgotten that and I try always, with varying success (especially when I am not quite sure what I want to say) to avoid polysyllabic verbiage.

It is one thing to learn how to use words, however long that may take, and however painful it may be. It is quite another matter to be a writer, to have something to say and to want to say it badly enough to get down to that blank foolscap. I doubt if this can be taught at all. You have, perhaps, like a painter or any other creative artist, to be born with it.

With only a natural impulse to write, not enough compulsion to do so, and with very poor equipment, I had to learn the hard way, discovering, through failure, more and more about the kind of writer that I can never be.

I began with a short story. It was written in a flat in Chelsea, in 1928, when I was 'beachcombing' at the Colonial Office. The only amusement we could afford in that freezing winter was to walk to the Royal Court Theatre in Sloane Square, sit in the pit, and choose either to eat chocolates in the interval or walk home. In those days the bookstalls were covered with magazines in much greater variety than now. The *Wide World*, the *Windsor*, the *Fortnightly*, the *Cornhill*, and half a dozen others were all looking for more literary essays or stories. Dorothy L. Sayers, A. J. Cronin, Agatha Christie, and Edgar Wallace all began by writing for the *Strand*. So, having somehow to pay the rent, I sat down one night to tell the story of *Mishoro Monty*, a man-eating lion which had killed over a hundred people while we were at Fort Jameson. The story was autobiographical and true, but it was my first literary child and it had a difficult birth. In particular, I remember trying to describe a night which I had spent with an Italian engineer and a white Rhodesian schoolboy up on a platform in a tree. We were waiting for the lion to return to the place under the tree where he had half eaten the body of a woman that afternoon. Mishoro Monty came, but he knew we were there and so he sat down a hundred yards away in the darkness and roared at us for three hours or more. His roars echoed down a rocky stream-bed below our tree. The whole dark frightened world trembled about us. When the moon rose he went away, and as his roars faded into the distance the trees stole silently out of the darkness and the moonlight lay listening on the grass.

Even now the memory is vivid enough, but when I came to write the story, six months after it happened, in that Chelsea flat with the seagulls wheeling at the windows and the tugs hooting on the river in the November fog, I could remember every detail of that long night except the exact sound of the coughs with which the lion ended each of his great roars. They were, I knew, of the very essence of the story and I ended up crawling about the floor trying out lion-noises on my year-old son until his laughter turned to shrieks. I would have done better to sit quietly and listen. It is only by listening that the right word comes, not from struggling and experiment.

The *Wide World* not only took the story but put me in glorious colours on the cover. I was in a pith helmet (I never owned one) aiming with the wrong sort of rifle at a roaring lion (which I had never myself seen). But they paid me £36 for it. This was wealth. We were made!

I promptly wrote several more stories, all based on my experiences in Africa. Some, in more thoughtful vein, on problems. They all sold.

Then Lovat Dickson, later of Macmillans but at that time starting to publish on his own, asked me to write a novel of African life. He, for his part, said he would first publish my stories as a book. This we called *Africa Notwithstanding*. Unfortunately, the title, when printed on the spine of the book, read:

AFRICA NOTWITHSTANDING KENNETH BRADLEY

It took me years to live that down in Northern Rhodesia. I am sure Lovat Dickson enjoyed the joke as much as everybody else did. I hope he did, because I was, and still am, so grateful to him

H

for encouraging me to spend many happy and agonizing hours during the rest of my life struggling to write as well and as usefully as he hoped I could.

I wrote more than half my novel for him, which was called *Hawks Alighting*, after the old Ngoni war cry,[1] on a fourteen-day voyage from Southampton to Cape Town. It was a story about a young Ngoni boy who went south to meet civilization. It was really a study in race-relations. Nobody was worrying very much about race-relations in 1929 and the study, if it can be called that, did not amount to much.

A few years later I tried again. This time the novel was to be a real literary effort, not about Africa at all. My wife and I were alone at Mumbwa, a hundred miles from anywhere. Every evening, after the children had been put to bed, we used to sit on opposite sides of the dining-room table in the pool of light spread by the Aladdin lamp between us, scribbling away. Neither of our novels even reached the typing stage, let alone a publisher. This was not surprising because we were writing in a vacuum, far removed from any contact with the outside world, gilding memories already distorted by time and distance. There were no road-drills outside, only the crickets chirruping in the deceptive quiet of the moonlit bush.

My story, I seem to remember, was a lyrical romance about Guernsey, where I had been so happy as a boy. It was florid, sentimental and adjectival. It was terrible.

Having thrown it all into the waste-paper basket, I faced up to the fact that I was not a novelist. I had set about it the wrong way, by choosing the lovely scene, thinking of a plot, and then trying to fit the characters into them. One must begin with the people or they emerge only as faceless puppets, or worse, nowadays, psychological and sociological types or, worse still, voices with messages. Compton Mackenzie, if I remember rightly, was hardly more successful with his own novel about his particular Channel Island.

People were not as vivid and real to me as places and things. I could not penetrate into their hearts and minds and therefore I

[1] *Adza Kaluangwe*. See p. 43.

could not make them come alive. Before this abortive effort and shortly after Lovat Dickson had published my first two books, and perhaps because of them I was, while still in the Secretariat at Livingstone, taken away from files and told to write a big book about Northern Rhodesia, including its history and anything else I could think of which might interest people. I enjoyed doing that, especially as I was given some extra leave to enable me to sit in the Rhodes House library at Oxford doing research. The result was indeed a large book. Unfortunately, the onset of the great depression caused the financial axe to fall upon it and the type-script still lies, mostly unpublished, in the Zambian archives. The historical part of it did in fact appear later as a series of articles in a magazine called the *African Observer*, published in Bulawayo. I rather wish it had not, because my shortcomings were exposed in later years to the scornful eyes of professional historians and social anthropologists. When I was writing they had not yet put in an appearance and everything in and about Central Africa, for lack of them, had still to be done by amateurs, including the writing of its history.

In 1935 I was called in from Mumbwa to Lusaka and given ten days in which to write a small book describing the new-built capital, of which copies were to be presented to all the distin-guished guests who were coming to attend the formal opening of the new capital. When the great day came, my wife, lucky girl, was already staying in Lusaka. She went to the ball and saw the fireworks, but I was not there. I spent the day sitting, in my best suit, on the landing-strip out at Mumbwa, waiting for an aero-plane which did not come. I had been invited to the celebrations and promised a plane. Labour troubles, alas, had suddenly threatened on the Copperbelt, all planes were needed for emergency duties and, of course, there was no way to let me know.

So, having discovered by 1938 that I was neither a writer of fiction nor an historian, but still wanting to write something, somehow, I found myself completely at a loss. Then, just when things were at their very worst, and no doubt because they were, the answer was given to me.

On the first evening of one *ulendo* after returning to Fort Jameson, I was sitting by my fire under a large wild fig-tree, relaxed and happy to be freed at last from the bondage of files and policies. Suddenly I wanted to describe the colours pulsating in the heart of the fire and the sound of the leaves of the tree above rustling in the rising heat. I reached for a pen and the first thought which came was that I would try to describe not just the fire's glow and the under-lit pattern of leaves dancing against the dark sky, but everything I had seen and done since I left Fort Jameson that morning.

Two hours and five pages later, having written down all that had happened during the day, I was back where I had started, staring at the fire and ready to describe it, but the glow had died and the leaves were still. I read what those hours' absorption had produced, added a word or two — about the camp and the fig-tree — and decided that I would do this every evening. I would write a diary of the whole *ulendo*.

I was now, almost for the first time, under a real compulsion to write, and I had something to say. I realized, and I do not know why I had not done so long ago, that the day-to-day experiences of a District Officer touring in Central Africa, though humdrum to him, were unlike anything else in the world and had never been described by anybody. And the bailiffs were at the door — not mine, but outside 27 Park Town, Oxford, where my wife was hoping somehow to pay the boys' fees at the Dragon School. *Blackwood's Magazine* might take one of the diaries, or two, or even a series. The bailiffs would not get through the door!

I sat down and wrote every night on that first *ulendo* and every night on every other *ulendo* I did during the next six months. I had decided, on the first evening, to write a diary strictly for publication. It must be a disciplined, literary exercise, which might bring Africa to life for people who did not know it, and not be merely a series of notes sufficient to bring it back to life for me in later years. A second decision was that it would not describe my work, except in so far as that formed the warp and woof of the day's pattern. I wanted to be free to try to evoke as clearly as I could the sight and sound and smells of Africa and the people as they were in themselves, not seen, blurred and distorted, through my official spectacles.

It was always so hard to remember that it was we and not they who were obsessed with their sociological problems. They were just people who took life as they found it, really only concerned with their private loves and hates, village gossip, hunting, food, sleep and that the birds or the elephants were eating the millet in the gardens. Nor was the thickly inhabited countryside just a series of problems in land-use. The hills were aloof and beautiful and the feathered grasses on the worked-out lands shone silver in the moonlight.

So, for better or for worse, few problems such as I have described in this book were mentioned in the *Diary*. At the time I was glad that it should be so because I found a wholly new delight both in the discipline of wrenching my mind away from my work and in the release of looking about me with a new awareness. Nearly all of us walk through the fields not only in gloves, but in blinkers, too. It was only now, when I knew that I must sit down in the evening, and put everything I had seen into words, that I pulled the blinkers off and tried to see. It is one thing to pass in front of a great tree and notice that it is beautiful. It is quite another to stand and study it, trying to see exactly why it is so and, in that same moment, not later in recollection, to listen for the exact words which will describe it. The need to see so clearly and to listen so keenly day after day as we wandered from village to village through the bush opened up for me a new intensity of living, with the eyes, imagination and mind all hard at work. Then, in the evenings, while the images of things seen were still clear-cut, the words came back without being called, and sheet after sheet of paper was filled with hardly a scratching-out. The writing was not a labour. It was easy and exciting.

Best of all were the evenings when what had to be described was actually happening around me. There was the night down in the Luangwa Valley when I could listen to elephant trumpeting half a mile away in the dark forest and write down the terrible sound of it while the hairs on the back of my neck were still prickling.

I remember another, very different evening at a village remotely perched on top of a pass in the border hills, when I was sitting at my table watching the sunset slowly turn the grey of a rocky crag to gold. Suddenly three pink pigs raced through the camp chased by three small, black, naked boys and all of them finished up in the cooking-hut in a whirlwind of saucepans, squeals and laughter.

Perhaps one recipe for learning to write is first to learn to use your eyes and then to record what you have seen with them, because with seeing comes understanding. Making a pattern of it is an art. I dare say that getting into the skin of other people and their relationships makes fiction and plays. This has always eluded me.

Month by month the instalments of the *Diary* went home to the Colonial Office for the official scrutiny required by the regulations, and month by month my wife harried the long-suffering officials into swift release of the typescript so that *Blackwood's* and the school bills should not be kept waiting.

Later, when I was on leave in Guernsey in the summer of 1939, I decided to turn idleness to profit by adding one more instalment. I wanted to describe, in the old diary form, how we had built the Ngoni school the year before. All the other instalments, written as direct reporting, had been so easy. Not so this last one, dragged up from memory. I had to rewrite it five times before I got it right, and even now it smells of the lamp and the blackout.

Later, during the war when we were in the Falkland Islands, the *Diary of a District Officer* was published as a book and over a hundred thousand copies of it were sold in a few months. Then, alas, no more paper could be made available and that was that. It was republished in 1947 at the request of Sir Ralph Furse, who wanted it as a bait to catch recruits for the Colonial Service, which had been much depleted by the war. It had, he said, the merit of being at once factual and romantic! It showed that I enjoyed my life, including the hardships of darkest Africa, so mysterious and daunting to the ignorant, and I had not minded saying so. Long afterwards I met a man who said he had read it in an aeroplane high over India on his way to Burma and that he said to himself there and then, 'When this war is over that is the life for me.' He was too polite to accuse me of seducing or misleading him. Now of course, the book is out of print, and out of date except as a contemporary record of the years of British imperial rule in Africa, a little period piece.[1] One day, since it was at least accurate, it may, I hope, be useful to some historian, though I did not know, when I was scribbling away beside those campfires, that I was in fact recording the end of an era.

I had learned at last what kind of writer I was, a reporter, and I was glad to know this truth, just as I was glad to have been taught that I was a District Officer and not a potential Colonial Secretary. My only regret was that I had not started to turn my *ulendos* into money-spinners long before at Mazabuka and Mumbwa. However, at least I could now look forward to blissful years administering Fort Jameson and writing by my firelit tent in perfect contentment. How wrong I was!

The war came and, all because of the *Diary*, I was never to go on another *ulendo* in Africa again. I was now presumed to be a writer and I was therefore immediately seconded to Headquarters as Information Officer. I spent the next three years writing everything, from articles to radio sketches, everything except reporting. After that I was to spend the rest of my Colonial Service career in Secretariats for which everyone, including me, had already decided that I was totally unsuited.

It is nice to start out on life on tramlines laid down for you by background and education, but they are not to be relied upon. Sooner or later, just when you have settled down and are beginning to enjoy the ride, you come to an unexpected junction and, before you know where you are, you find yourself careering off in a quite different direction on lines that do not fit your wheels, and leading to heaven knows where. That is when, with luck, the fun starts all over again.

[1] Macmillans are now, I am glad to say, republishing it.

CHAPTER 10

Information Officer

WE were on leave in Guernsey in the summer of 1939 when war was declared. A few weeks later I went to London to help my mother pile her furniture in the middle of her flat before she was evacuated. I also attended a course at the Colonial Office for which I had put my name down earlier in the summer. It had to do with labour relations in Africa and it had seemed relevant to our work with the tobacco planters of Fort Jameson. I had become interested in this subject two years earlier when I had accompanied G. St. C. Orde Browne, the first Labour Adviser to the Colonial Office, on a tour of Northern Rhodesia. He was a very large man and I was very small, and our little aeroplane had always flown with a sideways tilt which was rather alarming as we bounced low between the uninhabited hills or, spotting crocodiles on the sandbanks, skimmed the surface of the Zambezi.

Now, in September 1939, the course no longer seemed to have any relevance or importance at all. In any case, I only attended the first day of it because I was then sent for and told that I could neither be released for the army, nor return to Fort Jameson. The Colonial Office wanted me to go out to Lusaka immediately to start an Information service, whatever that might mean, for the Northern Rhodesia Government.

The Ministry of Information itself had just been set up in London and, while it was feeling its way into the distasteful field of propaganda, it was the target for much abuse and ribald comment. It made, indeed, a splendid target because there were as yet hardly any experts in psychological warfare, and it had to be staffed by the hurried recruitment of authors, dons, critics and other amateurs.

Northern Rhodesia, on a very small scale, was in the same dilemma. It had no experts in propaganda, and I was apparently the only amateur available who had ever published anything. Now I disliked propaganda as heartily as anyone else and the prospect of dedicating myself to it for the duration of the war was not attractive. However, it was clearly a job which had to be done by someone. At least it would be a more direct contribution to the war effort than trying to keep Fort Jameson happy.

They asked me if I had not better go along to the Ministry of Information and be taught how to do the job, but this was too much for my overwrought feelings. 'How not to do it, you mean!' I grumbled, and asked for passages to be booked to Africa on the next available boat.

So, since this was no time for families to be separated, in October we sailed, all four of us. By mid-November we were back in Lusaka.

It seemed that the Colonial Office had told the Northern Rhodesian Government it ought to have an Information Officer. Nobody in Lusaka had ever heard of such a creature before or had any idea of what he was supposed to do. They were also very busy putting the country on a war footing and had more important things to think about. So they gave me two rooms and a steno-grapher and asked for suggestions.

The problem was not so much knowing what to do as how to do it. The nearest enemy was several thousand miles away, so there was no necessity nor opportunity for attacking him with the meretricious weapons of psychological warfare. Our job would be to maintain the morale and encourage the war effort of both Africans and Europeans in Northern Rhodesia. The Europeans would be relying for news of the war on the B.B.C., and all we could hope to do was to supplement the meagre resources of the two small local newspapers with additional pictures and articles sent out from the Ministry of Information. This would not amount to very much, nor present much difficulty.

It might well be more important and much more difficult to keep the Africans fully informed. There was one African news-paper published weekly by the Government in English and several African languages. It was called, ironically enough,

Mutende, meaning 'Peace' or 'Greetings', which are pleasantly synonymous in some of the local languages. Such a paper could be increased in size, fed with a constant supply of material and distributed more widely throughout the country. This would hardly be enough. A broadcasting service? No Africans had any receivers and very few could afford to buy them.

In addition to keeping people informed about the war itself it would also be necessary to keep them informed about the policies of the Government. How was all this to be done with such a meagre press and no other means of communication except the District Commissioners? They could not be expected to spend their time calling meetings all over their Districts. The means of communication must be improved.

This was a slow process, but during the next few months we did begin to feed the local European press; we did enlarge *Mutende* both in size and distribution; and we did start our own short-wave broadcasting station. Later we began to publish our own weekly news-sheet for free distribution. When the Northern Rhodesia Regiment went away on active service we made another one for them, full of home news. By the end of 1941 our staff had grown to five, all of them wives of men who were away at the war. I found myself dictating about ten thousand words a week for articles, communiqués, feature programmes, sketches and news bulletins for the radio.

None of us had ever had any experience either in journalism or in broadcasting. I did not even own a radio. We had no one to advise us and nobody, so far as we knew, had ever before tried broadcasting to Africans. However, I had spent the past ten years, as had the District Officer husbands of most of our staff, doing pioneer work of one sort or another without much money and in trying to explain its value to Africans. Now we would only be trying to do the same thing with different media. It was not so difficult after all.

Nor was it often difficult to handle the news of the war. Most of the older Africans in the villages had served as soldiers or porters in the East African campaign in the First World War. It is odd to think now that they called Tanzania 'German East'. I remember how highly they respected the German *askari* and how much they despised their own allies from the Congo, who, they said, used to eat the corpses after a battle. These veterans and their children regarded the 'Geremani' as traditional enemies whom it was natural to fight again, and the more sophisticated people in the towns were wholly with us. There was no disloyalty to combat, only moments of distressed astonishment when the Allies suffered a defeat. Always we told the truth, according to the gospel of the B.B.C., in so far as we knew it. If we had not, and had tried to gloss over set-backs and disasters, we could not have lived with ourselves and we should also have floundered from lie to lie into ever worse confusion. Honesty was not only the best, but the only possible policy.

The other side of our work, explaining the policies and actions of our own Government, was far more difficult, not, as one might think, because we were asked to put over unconvincing explanations of doubtful policies or clumsy actions, but because it was almost impossible to persuade the officials to tell us what the policies were or what they were doing about them.

This clam-like reticence of the Government was in such sharp contrast to the constant publicity given to political affairs in any developed country that it needs some explanation. The main reason for it was that in Northern Rhodesia twenty years ago the country was governed by Civil Servants, who shun publicity, and not by politicians, who need it. The only politicians of any sort were amateurs among the Europeans, whose elected representatives were in a permanent minority in the Legislative Council. They influenced policy but they did not make it. We Civil Servants used to claim that, although a colonial Government was not democratic and had little fire in its belly, it could at least be relied on to try to decide every issue on its merits. This would certainly not be the case once party politics had taken over. We all realized that, sooner or later, political development was inevitable. We conscientiously and steadily promoted it in African tribal government, as an educational exercise, but we honestly felt that the growth of political democracy would add nothing to the happiness of the people, which was our chief concern. We thought that it should and could be developed slowly and surely, keeping pace with the spread of education.

I sympathized with the reluctance of Heads of Departments to tell me what they were doing. I remembered how as a D.C. I had never told anyone about my experiments unless and until they were successful. The Africans in those days did trust the Government. If it had then got into the habit of explaining its policies to the people in advance, instead of justifying them as *faits accomplis*, a new, more candid relationship might have grown up which would have greatly helped in the more difficult years to come.

All colonial Information Officers came to feel like this. As they became more expert in publicity techniques their own professional faith in the value of publicity naturally grew stronger. In 1940 they were strange and suspect and highly dangerous, voices crying in the wilderness. It took many years for them to be heard. All of which was perfectly understandable, and if I had still been District Commissioner, Fort Jameson, I too would no doubt have been saying with all the others: 'Leave explanations to your D.C.s as you have always done. We know our people.'

As I have said, the point was that the District Commissioners did not have any technical media of communication — newspapers, printed broadsheets, and broadcasting — and we had. It is also fair to say that once we had developed these media, the District Commissioners were glad to make good use of them. They put radio receivers and loudspeakers wherever there were enough people to listen to them, and they were enthusiastic distributors of *Mutende* and all our other publications.

In those early days we were chiefly interested in learning the techniques of the job and in setting up our broadcasting station. This was all new and it was all fun. For my part, I had to learn how to edit articles, hand-outs and news items; how a newspaper (only a very small one) is put together, and how to write articles in simple English and broadcast scripts for Africans about everything from the fall of Tobruk to improved methods of cultivating maize.

In learning how to write simply, I was fortunate enough, quite early in the war, to be given the opportunity to write two little textbooks for African schools. One was a short *Story of Northern Rhodesia*. The other described the African courts and authorities through which tribal self-government was being fostered. Both these little books were written in Basic English — or at least they would have been, if the experts had yet produced their Basic English vocabulary. In fact, our African Education Department had to invent its own, choosing two or three hundred of the most common English words. Writing these two little books was a splendid exercise in simplicity, made easier by years of experience in talking to Africans who had only a little knowledge of English. Both books continued to be used in Northern Rhodesian schools for twenty years, and the annual trickle of royalties has only recently dried up.

The really exciting adventure, however, was starting the broadcast service for Africans. The first thing, obviously, was to make sure, since no Africans had their own receivers, that we should have an audience. District Commissioners, missionaries, the mining companies and others all promised to co-operate. In the huge African townships on the Copperbelt clusters of loudspeakers were hung on the trees and thousands of people gathered round them to hear the evening bulletins. Officials, settlers and missionaries far out in the bush took their receivers out on to their verandas and turned the volume knobs full on to let the African drumming, which was our call-sign, draw listeners from the compounds and near-by villages. They would come silently, one by one, or in families, through the trees and stand and listen outside the mosquito wire, the whites of their eyes and their teeth gleaming in the darkness. In many homes the house-servants came into the sitting-room to listen. It was up to us to provide the programmes.

We set up our studio in a small, unoccupied room in the airport building, and draped the walls and windows with thick brown blankets to keep out some of the noise of the aircraft. We had a small, short-wave transmitter about a mile away, which was operated by a Post Office engineer. Three African teachers were recruited from a local school to act as translators and broadcasters in their own languages. Thus equipped, we went on the air for an hour or so several evenings a week in English and three African languages with a special all-English programme on Sundays.

We began modestly with bulletins of war and local news and official announcements interspersed with records of European and African music, each programme being repeated in the four languages. Later, as our confidence grew, we added sketches and little feature programmes of our own devising and were also able to use a number of programmes and talks sent out to us on records from London.

It was hard work, because I not only had to write every word of our own programmes myself, but I also had to produce them, do all the announcing and operate all the controls in the studio. I used to sit in front of the control panel, with two gramophone turntables and a microphone, conducting a kind of one-man band, announcing, reading scripts, twiddling knobs and changing records. Our three African broadcasters took it in turn to sit at another microphone across the room, and throughout this always hectic performance I had to listen in my earphones to see how, if at all, we were coming over on the air.

Only too often we were not on the air at all, either because one of the airport mechanics had turned off the main switch, which was in the hangar, or because something went wrong with the transmitter, or, on one memorable occasion, because the engineer abandoned his post in the middle of a thunderstorm. 'Hi!' he yelled at me on the telephone when I was reading a news bulletin and trying to make myself heard over the crashing thunderclaps. 'This machine is giving out blue sparks. I'm off. I'm closing down.' And so we did, when I was in the middle of a sentence.

With such primitive arrangements and a service operated by people not one of whom had ever been inside a broadcasting studio in his life, the only thing to do was to exploit our amateurishness and make the most of it. If, for instance, a bomber started to take off outside on its way to the North African front, I would say into the microphone, 'You hear that aeroplane? Let's wait until it's gone.' I remember how a nightjar came out of the darkness one night to sit on the window-sill and screech. I stopped broadcasting my talk on the day's news, took the microphone over to the window and broadcast the bird instead. This kind of thing went down very well with our listeners, both European and African, and we became quite popular as the most 'human' station on the air.

In this we were greatly helped by our African teacher-announcers, who took to the microphone as naturally as they did to their classrooms and talked to their unseen listeners as simply and sympathetically as they did to their own pupils. One of them proved to be a comedian too. Sometimes between us we wrote and produced little sketches for African consumption, and more than once this man with his inspired ad-libbing had us all laughing so much that nothing but giggles came over. The African listeners enjoyed that, too, because with them laughter is immediately infectious.

I remember, too, one Easter Service when the Bishop of Northern Rhodesia came and talked. A girl in the Secretariat who had a sweet, pure voice, was persuaded to sing Gounod's *Ave Maria*. In the post a few days later came a postcard from a tobacco planter in Southern Rhodesia asking whether it had been sung by Melba and could he have the number of the record? Never was a girl more pleased.

It was difficult to persuade the more Very Important Persons in the Government to come and broadcast. They had never done it and they were nervous. Africans, on the other hand, had no such inhibitions. On one occasion I arrived outside the studio to find sitting there a little group of elderly men and young girls. They were all in loin-cloths, and they had walked over a hundred miles from some remote village. They wanted to come and sing on the 'little box' which they had heard at their local mission. They were rather shy and shuffled their bare feet in the red dust, and one of the girls was giggling behind her hand. She had polished her pretty self from head to toe with castor oil for the occasion and had put a little green comb in her hair. We took them into the studio and while they stood quietly waiting round their microphone, we described them and the manner of their arrival to our listeners and wished them luck. At my signal they burst into song and, all nervousness vanished, gave a beautiful performance.

Our greatest triumph, however, was a special programme which we put on for the benefit of a District Officer who was conducting a recruiting campaign for the army in a group of villages about seventy miles away. He had a receiver and loud-speaker with him, and we had promised to put on this special programme in the evening, when he would have assembled some hundreds of people to listen to it. We had arranged the pro-gramme carefully, with a pep-talk by a sergeant-major, martial music, records of African war-dances and so on, but it all had to be rearranged because, when we arrived at the studio, there, standing outside the door was a tiny little man. He was a midget, not more than four feet tall. He saluted smartly.

'May I speak to my mother on the little box?'

'Where is she?'

'She is in the village where the *Bwana* has gone to find soldiers for the army.'

'How did you know we were going to do a special broadcast to that village?'

'Oh — I knew.' — The bush-telegraph had been at work. — 'I want to speak to her. I was a cook with the First Battalion of the Northern Rhodesia Regiment when it was fighting the Italians in Somaliland. I have only today come back and my mother believes that I was killed. I want to tell her that I am alive.'

So we ushered him into the studio and during the programme we stood him up on a box so that he could speak into the tall microphone and told him to call his mother.

'Mother?' he said, in the most casual voice. 'Is my mother there, the wife of Alamu? I am your son Adam. I have not been killed. I am coming home.' He stood down, happy, serene as ever, and we went on with the programme.

A few days later the District Officer wrote to me. As soon as Adam's voice came out of the darkness into the hush of that great gathering, there was, he said, a deep shuddering sigh. Then a woman, perhaps his mother, shrieked, 'A spirit! It is a spirit! It is the spirit of Adam, who is dead!' For a few seconds more they all sat there on the ground, the whites of their frightened eyes shining in the firelight. Then they rose and fled. Every man,

woman and child stampeded into the dark forest. But after a few
minutes they began to come out of the trees again, still frightened,
a little bit ashamed, and very excited. At that moment, it seems,
we in the studio, were starting to play records of Zulu war-dances,
and as they continued I, to heighten their effect, was gradually
increasing their speed.

This, I was afterwards told, was almost too much for the
young men and girls. They all began to sing and dance and stamp
in a rising frenzy. Nearly a hundred men were recruited by Adam
for the army on that famous night, but he himself had slipped
out of the studio and I never saw him again. No doubt he went
home to the village and laughed at all his friends, especially at
those who had in their excitement signed on for the army and gone
away to the war from which he himself had so happily escaped.

By the middle of 1942 our little staff had grown quite expert,
and very tired. Each day, for week after week and month after
month, had had its stint of newsletters, news bulletins, articles
and sketches. I myself was written out. For nearly three years I
had been pouring out words, words and more words. Hundreds
of thousands of them. All written or dictated at speed to meet ever-
pressing deadlines. No time for precision, no time for style, no
time for new thinking or indeed for very much thought of any
kind. I had indeed become a hack and I had gone completely
stale. Better writers than I have suffered from this at one time or
another. Some of them, no doubt, have never been able fully to
recover from the damage it did. Even now, twenty years later, I
find that the pen runs on too easily, too quickly, too thoughtlessly.
Always I am haunted by a deadline and if there is no deadline, I
invent one. Ideas do not come and must be given to me by
others. I can think of few things I have written since I left Lusaka
more than twenty years ago which have not been commissioned
or suggested by someone else, including this book. This is a great
frustration.

But, for the first two years, those script-driven relentless days
were enjoyable, especially after some of my friends fell for the
lure of the microphone and volunteered to help with the
broadcasting.

Lusaka was growing up and putting on sophistication, but it did keep much of the social ease and friendliness which were our Rhodesian heritage. We all had a very good time. When I went back there for a few days early in 1964, I even found myself a little homesick for it. Surprisingly, the airport building looked much the same. I could see the door of our old studio. The great hangar was still there, and my heart turned over as we taxied up to it because in front of it was standing a little sunburned boy in khaki shirt and shorts watching the aeroplanes, just as my younger son had done when he was ten.

Now, of course, they have a Broadcasting Corporation and are very professional. The man who had taken over the broadcasting from me in 1942 and had developed the famous receiver for Africans known as the 'saucepan radio' because it would fit into a cooking-pot, and had built up the service to professional standards, was now one of its Governors. We amused ourselves, if nobody else, for half an hour, recording reminiscences of those quite forgotten days. A Rip Van Winkle is subject to strange temptations, as when I opened the door into our old Information Office and found it still occupied by five young women, all typing busily. 'But you ought to be five grass widows', I said, and, as I softly closed the door behind me, all the typewriters stopped. If I grew a beard it would be almost white.

To return, however, to 1942. One morning, when I was sitting, staring dumbly at my secretary, bled white and unable even to begin dictating the daily stint, the door opened and in walked the Chief Secretary. 'Would you', he said, 'like to go to the Falkland Islands as Colonial and Financial Secretary?'

The Falklands? Where, in the wide world, were they? Africa was my world, and I did not want another. Colonial Secretary? But everyone knew that I was no good as a Secretariat man. They had told me so. Financial Secretary? When it had taken me two years to learn to keep a cashbook? 'Let me know tomorrow', he said.

There were, in the Northern Rhodesian Service at any rate, two schools of thought about transfers. One said, 'Never refuse an opportunity. Once you start moving you keep on moving and it is always upwards.' My uncle, too, had told me, nearly twenty years before, never to refuse an opportunity. The other school said, 'Don't move. No one who has accepted a transfer from Northern Rhodesia has ever been so happy anywhere else.' There is truth in both these views. It is never simply a choice between ambition and contentment; there are always other factors. A transfer to a strange country and a strange Service is always a challenge. It may also be an escape from a boss whom you dislike or a job which bores you. It may, or may not, be of benefit to your wife and children. It nearly always means more pay and the possibility of settling that overdraft once and for all. It is always a temptation.

The job was no doubt being hawked round the colonies to see if anyone would be foolish enough to take it. Our elder boy was at school in Natal. The younger ought to be going down there, too, next year. How could they be dragged off to the Falklands where there were probably no schools at all? Could I leave my family in South Africa and put the wide Atlantic between us in the middle of a war?

Nevertheless, it was a challenge. It was, above all, an escape. I was written out. This I knew and this, no doubt, was why the transfer had been offered to me.

My wife and I talked it over all the evening and I lay awake through the small hours seeing visions of the snow-peaked Andes, of spouting whales and great green seas, of escape into a whole new world where everything would be strange. No more heat, no more dust, no more scripts, no more deadlines. Escape. The 'magic casements' were opening for the second time, wider and wider as the small hours ticked by. By morning I knew that I must go through them.

At some point in his working life a decision like this has to be made by almost every man, when his job seems to demand that he should uproot himself and his family from their home and start another one somewhere else. The choice is always difficult and the circumstances are never the same. We still do not know whether the decision we took in 1942 was the right one.

We had a short and very happy family holiday in a cottage on the coast of Natal and then I sailed for the Falklands in June. The others stayed behind. Both the boys would be at school at Pietermaritzburg, and my wife was going to teach at a near-by girls' school. I was to go ahead and reconnoitre and, if it seemed right, they were to follow me in a year's time.

CHAPTER II

The Falklands and the Antarctic

THE last three years of the war we spent as far away from it as it was possible to be, in utterly remote surroundings completely different from Africa. I have often thought of my time in the Falklands as an irrelevant interlude, but now I am not so sure. Three years of entirely new experiences must have their effect on any man.

They began in Africa, for I sailed from Durban in an Argentine ship, the *José Menendez*. When I reached the top of the gangway, lugging suitcases, the chief officer said to me,

'You go to *las Malvinas*, no?'

'I'm going to the Falklands', I answered, short of breath.

'Same thing. *Las Malvinas sono Argentinas*. After the war — you will see.' Only one of the ship's officers spoke to me again on the whole voyage.

This was the first I had ever heard of the Argentine's claim to the Falklands which was pressed so hard during the régime of Peron, when Britain was busy with the war. It still makes occasional, very small headlines in our newspapers.

Only recently, in 1964, a dashing young Argentine pilot flew his little plane across hundreds of miles of gale-torn sea to land on the little racecourse in the Falklands, plant the Argentine flag there and fly away again before anybody could stop him. A fine piece of impertinence.

The claim goes a long way back into history. The islands were probably first sighted by John Davies, an Englishman, master of the *Desire*, in 1592. Two years later they were visited by John Hawkins, who found them uninviting and uninhabited and sailed away again. Nobody seems to have gone near them again for a hundred and fifty years or more. Then the French came and built a fort on East Falkland. They sold out to the Spaniards and the

British promptly sent a small party out to build a fort of their own on West Falkland. They claimed the islands through right of discovery. The Spaniards claimed them through right of occupation and said they were Spanish; in any case, had not Pope Julius II in 1592 issued a Bull allotting all undiscovered land in that part of the world to Spain? An argument unlikely to appeal to heretic England. To make their point, the Spaniards drove the British out. This made Whitehall very angry. Edmund Burke thundered in Parliament, and there was very nearly a war. The Spaniards gave way, and British soldiers reoccupied West Falkland. That all happened in 1770. But the British disliked the place exceedingly and saw no future for it, so almost at once they sailed away. The Spaniards left, too, before very long, and the islands were left once more to the penguins and the winds.

Nothing more happened until 1820, when the Spanish colonial government in Buenos Aires gave a concession in the islands to a Frenchman called La Fone, and he founded a settlement on East Falkland. At that time sealers were going south in large numbers and were busy exterminating the fur-seal population. The Argentine settlers dealt rather severely with one of these men, an American, and not long after, in 1831, an American warship, the U.S.S. *Lexington*, arrived to investigate. Her captain burned down the settlement and deported the settlers back to the Argentine, which was now independent.

When, for the second time, the British came to hear that impudent foreigners had been occupying one of their possessions which they had forgotten all about, they determined to put a stop to such goings-on once and for all. Marines arrived to occupy Port Stanley and found the islands once more deserted, except for herds of white cattle which had belonged to the Argentine settlers and which were now running wild in the hills. Civil government was established in 1841, and in the years that followed nearly all the land in the colony was sold off in huge tracts to enterprising British wool-farmers. Much of it now belongs to the Falkland Islands Company, and they and the descendants of the other settlers have been doing very well out of wool ever since.

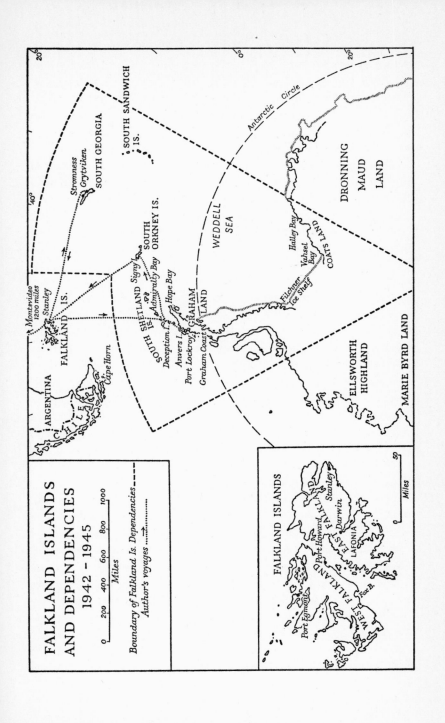

FALKLAND ISLANDS
AND DEPENDENCIES
1942 - 1945

Miles
0   200   400   600   800   1000

Boundary of Falkland Is. Dependencies -----
Author's voyages ....

FALKLAND ISLANDS

WEST FALKLAND
Port Egmont
Fox B.
Port Howard
Darwin
Stanley
EAST FALKLAND
LAFONIA

0   50
Miles

ARGENTINA
CHILE
Cape Horn
FALKLAND IS.
Stanley
Montevideo
1200 miles

SOUTH GEORGIA
Stromness
Grytviken
SOUTH SANDWICH IS.

SOUTH SHETLAND IS.
Deception I.
Anvers I.
Port Lockroy
Graham Coast
GRAHAM LAND
Hope Bay
Admiralty Bay
Signy I.
SOUTH ORKNEY IS.

WEDDELL SEA

Antarctic Circle

DRONNING MAUD LAND

Halley Bay
Vahsel Bay
COATS LAND
Filchner Ice Shelf

ELLSWORTH HIGHLAND

MARIE BYRD LAND

20°   0°   20°
40°
40°

Today there are about three thousand Falkland Islanders, of whom about half live in Stanley.

As the Falklands have been inhabited entirely by British people for more than a hundred years, nobody, except some nationalists in the Argentine, takes that country's claim very seriously, but it was to give us a lot of trouble during the nineteen-forties.

The S.S. *José Menendez* was filled with a polyglot collection of European refugees from Asia and the Middle East. There were French oil men from the Far East, and a Greek lawyer from the Levant with his classically beautiful peasant wife who never spoke and hardly knew how to use a knife and fork. There was a Jew from Poland who hoped to slip into the United States through Cuba and other people with as many adventures behind them as James Bond himself.

The ship was small and elegant. She had been designed to carry rich cattlemen up the Argentine coast from their vast *estancias* in Patagonia to civilization in Buenos Aires, but she was quite unsuited for rounding Cape Agulhas in a winter gale of horrific severity. 'It is not that I am frightened,' said the Greek lawyer as we saw a wall of green water rear over the bows, crash on the foredeck and hiss along the rails, 'but ships *do* break!'

After leaving Cape Town, where all the biggest ships in the world seemed to be gathered, taking the troops to Egypt who were to turn the tide of war at El Alamein, we beat our way out into the constant westerlies across four thousand miles of the South Atlantic. The baby grand piano and the spindly chairs in the locked *salon* slid, night and day, to and fro across the parquet floor, while the seas spattered against the boarded windows and marched past in never-ending blue-and-silver ranks. We averaged five knots all the way from Cape Town to the Plate. The tattered jib which was sometimes run up from the forecastle to give us extra speed could not have helped us much. The blue and white stripes of the Argentine flag painted on the hull were brilliantly floodlit, a protective advertisement which seemed rather perilous to all the 'belligerent' passengers. Some of them would have made valuable prisoners for the captain of a roving U-boat. The black dust acquired from the Durban coaling-wharf was never cleaned off. When the crew did have one boat-drill, none of the davits seemed to work. However, no enemy appeared and eventually we arrived, having seen no sign of life in all those four thousand miles, except, of course, one albatross.

I did not see Buenos Aires. I was not allowed to land there and was sent down-river to Montevideo that same night. This did not, I think, have anything to do with the Argentine's claim to *las Malvinas*, for none of the foreigners on the *José Menendez*, except the Americans, were allowed to land, although we had all paid for transit visas. Some of them spent days on board, prisoners in a coaling-dock. I was rescued by the British Consulate and hurried away under escort and seething with patriotic indignation, to the river-steamer, where I was locked into my cabin.

In charming contrast, at Montevideo I was wafted through immigration and customs — 'We make no formalities for our friends the English', they said — and when I walked into a shop to buy some cigarettes, the proprietor said, 'I sell nothing to the English. My shop is yours, Señor.' This, before El Alamein, when the fortunes of my country were so low, was balm indeed, and I could hardly speak to thank him.

Uruguay, with its nineteenth-century British trams, gasworks and railways (Montevideo station, the signals, the level-crossing gates and even the porters' uniforms took us straight home to Paddington and the Oxford run), had always been a staunch friend of ours. It also happens to be the best-ordered democracy in South America. That friendship had recently been strengthened by the Battle of the River Plate, which ended with the scuttling of the *Graf Spee* within sight of the waterfront at Montevideo and of great cheering crowds who had gone down to see the fun. In those days there was no love lost between little Uruguay and its giant neighbour the Argentine, where there were some 400,000 Germans and an unpredictable dictator.

By good fortune, the only ship which plied between Montevideo and the Falklands, and that only every two months or so, was in port when I arrived. We were ready to sail next day.

The S.S. *Fitzroy*, 400 tons, was, throughout the war, the only link, other than the radio, between the Falklands and the world.

It was strange, after three years in Africa and a month as the only Englishman on a South American ship, to go aboard this tiny, spotless little British vessel; to be greeted by her brisk captain with an English 'How d'you do'; to hear her red-cheeked, blue-jerseyed crew calling to each other in what sounded like a Berkshire accent, and to sit down to a meal of roast mutton, boiled potatoes and swedes.

Twelve hundred miles of the South Atlantic lie between Montevideo and the Falklands. They include the 'roaring forties', almost as notorious as the 'howling sixties', where giant seas sweep right round the bottom of the world south of the Horn, with half a mile between each foaming crest. Sailing in the *Fitzroy* through such seas during the next three years I came, if not to love, certainly to admire her. She was snub-nosed and short-tailed, with a tall funnel, which belched black smoke, and she was very small indeed. I was told that in those great seas it was better to travel in a slow, very small ship, which crawls up and over and down the waves, rather than in a faster, bigger ship which can easily mistime the seas and have to crash straight through them. This was true. The little *Fitzroy*, even in the most furious of gales, never shipped a sea. She just strolled up and over and down, wriggled at the bottom and climbed up again. To endure this, one had, of course, to be a very good sailor. This I am, and I soon discovered that it was much better to leave all one's belongings on the floor of the cabin, where they had all fallen, because nothing would stay put anywhere else. The captain was worried only by fog, icebergs and rocks. I came on deck one morning on a later voyage to South Georgia after a blissfully peaceful night when we had lain gently rolling with the thumping engines stilled, in a very thick fog. Now it was a cold, blue morning and an icy gale was tearing up from the south, driving dark, foam-crested seas before it. The captain was standing on the bridge, his blue eyes sparkling.

'This is the stuff!' he shouted, pushing the engine-telegraph over to Full Ahead. 'Now we can see them', and he pointed to a great green-and-silver berg hull down on the crinkled horizon. I heard somewhere that the *Fitzroy* ended her days on a reef off one of the Falkland Islands, but I hope that this is only a sailor's yarn.

On this first voyage, five days later in the early morning, we glimpsed through cold driving rain a white lighthouse and low-lying land. We slipped between rocky shores into a long, land-locked sound, to see little white and yellow houses climbing up a bare hillside and a distant frieze of rain-dimmed mountains black against dark cloud. This was Stanley, the capital city of the Falklands. If it had not been for the penguins which were escorting us through the Heads we might well have been somewhere in the Outer Hebrides.

The two main islands, East and West Falkland, are each about a hundred miles long and less than half as wide, and there are dozens of smaller islands clustering round them. The land is bleak — all bog, moorland and coarse yellow grass, broken by granite tors, rising on East Falkland to forbidding peaks of some five thousand feet. Outside Stanley, there are no roads, but only pony tracks along which the shepherds ride. The whole colony is divided up into great sheep ranches. Apart from one other sizeable settlement named after Darwin (he came that way in the *Beagle* more than a hundred years ago), the only signs of man in the great, wind-swept loneliness are occasional white ranch houses tucked into sheltered corners of the sea-lochs, and even more occasional shepherds' cottages.

In winter it rains, snows, freezes and thaws in alternating raw discomfort. In the summer, when there is more sun but little warmth, the perpetual winds blow stronger than ever. Yet, when there is — perhaps once in a month — a calm, sunny day, a glorious clear light shines on the white beaches and on the peacock iridescence of the seas, spouting in silver fountains on the dark rocks. On such crystal days we could count the posts in a fence a mile away and see the eagles soaring over the grey tors. Then I always allowed half of my staff in turn to have a holiday. One or two of them were hardy enough to bathe.

There never were any native inhabitants of the Falklands. The three thousand islanders there in my day were nearly all English, with a sprinkling of Scandinavians descended from the crews of whaling ships which gathered in Port Stanley in the olden days.

The idea that the islands are inhabited by Scotsmen is a myth.

The town of Stanley is a survival of Victorian England. There is a plethora of pubs, which sell draught English beer, and there is also a small cathedral. Government House is like an English country house with its walled garden and a disproportionately large conservatory. There are no trees, none at all, except for a few which have been planted in the shelter of houses or stone walls. These grow no taller than their shelter, for the salt winds shrivel their tops away. Every house in Stanley — all built of wood — has its own little glassed-in porch full of English flowers. Gorse and broom shine yellow in November, which is the southern spring.

It was strange to find these poignant reminders of home so far away beneath the curve of the world, as strange as it was, many years later, to find the Scottish border country recreated round Dunedin in the southern corner of New Zealand.

The islanders were not poor and their houses were warm and comfortable and very clean. They seemed to us to lead hard lives, out in every kind of abominable weather, riding the moors to watch over the wandering sheep and spending every long summer evening out on the hillsides cutting peat. There was no other fuel and in that climate fires had to be kept burning day and night throughout the year. They were slaves to the peat-bogs and I only hope that the dream I had of providing electric power for the whole of Stanley has now come true. One of the local girls who came to work for us could not understand why the people in war-time England suffered so much from the coal shortage. 'Why don't they burn their peat?' she asked. Then she married a soldier who was a Yorkshire miner and has probably spent the rest of her days in the shadow of his colliery.

Life on the sheep ranches could be very lonely, but was not always the worse for that. One young ex-officer and his wife had come out after the First World War and bought themselves one of the smaller islands off West Falkland. They had lived there ever since, educating their children and happy with their radio and supplies of books sent out from London. They did not come into Stanley while we were there and, so far as I know, had hardly left their island in twenty years.

There was also an elderly German who owned another very remote little island. He walked into my office one morning, just before VE Day. I asked him what he was doing in Stanley since he had been interned on his island ever since September 1939 and had no right to leave it without permission. He was very indignant. Not only, he protested, had he never heard of his internment, but, having been born in Danzig, which was a Free City, he was not even a German. Speechless, I gave him permission to go up to Montevideo for a holiday.

I treasure, too, a story told to us by the Bishop, who used to come and visit us from Buenos Aires. He had, he said, been to visit an old bedridden shepherd on West Falkland. He read to him the story of the Crucifixion, and when he closed his Bible he saw that the old man was crying. Surprised and moved he asked him why he was crying over the old, familiar story. 'Ah,' said the shepherd, 'you knew it, but I've never heard about it before. You see, we don't get any newspapers here.'

In Stanley itself there were about fifteen hundred people, nearly all of good British country stock, stubborn, conservative, enduring and, in spite of much intermarriage, strong. Everyone was cousin to somebody else — and they all talked with that flat Berkshire-like accent and called England 'home', though few of them had ever been there. Some of the men, when young, went to sea, but most of them came back. Now, in war-time, only a few were away, serving in the Royal and Merchant Navies, for most had been conscripted into the local Defence Force. They loved their island.

Stanley seemed a sad place, partly because of the bleak peat-bogs and hills and the winds which moaned about the chimney-pots and blurred the dark waters of the Sound, but mostly, I dare say, because it had been touched by greatness in the past and now had only memories. Not only Darwin had passed this way; so had Shackleton and other famous Antarctic explorers, and those fleets of whaling ships a hundred years ago and great four-masters from round the Horn.

At an old wooden jetty below our house lay the hulk of an East Indiaman on which boys played pirates. In a cove some miles

away still rested George Brunel's fam. us steamship the *Great
Britain*. She had finally reverted to sail, carrying emigrants to
Australia, and had ended her days here with only a penguin
rookery for company. Few ships ever drop anchor in Port
Stanley now.

The greatest day in the island's story, ever after kept as a holiday,
had been 8th December 1914, when Admiral Sturdee had sailed
out from Port Stanley and defeated a German squadron under
Admiral Von Spee in the Battle of the Falklands.

My cook had been the heroine of that famous day. She was a
young girl then, working as nursery maid for Mrs. Felton (now
Mrs. Creamer), on one of the sheep stations down the coast.
When she went up on to the windy hillside to hang the baby's
nappies on the line, there on the horizon she saw the sinister grey
shapes of the German warships steaming by. Down the hill she
ran, her dark hair flying in the wind, to tell her mistress 'Big ships,
going north, fast, and they ain't ours!' Mrs. Felton, the baby on
her knee, grabbed the telephone and wound the handle fiercely,
to get the news to Stanley. Our ships, lying in the harbour, were
coaling, all unready, but by the time the Germans were abreast of
the lighthouse they were out and ready to give chase. The engraved
teapot in our kitchen and the huge silver tray in Mrs. Creamer's
dining-room were tokens of gratitude from their Lordships of
the Admiralty. Fifty years later, in 1964, they still remembered
and presented Mrs. Creamer with a set of Falkland Islands stamps
specially issued to mark the golden jubilee of that never-to-be-
forgotten day.

What old memories must have stirred when, thirty-five years
later, the cruiser *Exeter* limped into Port Stanley after the Battle of
the River Plate, to put her wounded into our cottage hospital
and patch the holes in her shell-torn hull!

When I said good-bye to the young captain of the *Fitzroy*, he
said, 'Don't imagine that you're going to achieve anything here.
No Colonial Secretary ever has.' He was right.

They were absurd, really, those grandiose titles of the Colonial
Service — His Excellency the Governor, the Honourable the
Colonial Secretary, and all the rest of them — in these remote,

cold, little islands, with their English village capital. We were two men and a boy keeping the parish pump going. Not that this was easy in the middle of a war. What could we do, for instance, when the only dentist in the islands left and we could not get another? What could we do with one old lady whose wits deserted her and no family could bear to keep her in their home? The cottage hospital was not designed for noisy lunatics and she could not stay in the little prison for very long, however comfortable all three members of our police force made it for her. Yet there was very little to do, and since I am a bad 'maintainer' it was lucky for me that, as it turned out, most of my work did not lie in the familiar trivialities of administration but in quite new fields.

When I arrived I found that I had done so on the heels of a garrison of British troops. They had been sent out to protect the islands against a possible invasion by the Japanese, who, after they had destroyed the American fleet at Pearl Harbor, might conceivably make a two-pronged attack on the Panama Canal and the Horn Passage into the Atlantic. Churchill, after the loss of Singapore, was in no mood to allow even the smallest hair of the Lion's tail to be pulled out. How one battalion of infantry and ancillary service with a few Bofors guns could have protected the Falklands against an air and sea task-force was a strategic mystery. What we needed was a Sunderland or two to watch for the German blockade-runners which were using the Horn Passage, but we supposed, rightly, that there were none to spare. However, this was no concern of mine. My job was to keep the relations between the garrison and the islanders happy.

The fact that this turned out to be a sinecure was a great tribute both to the Yorkshiremen who garrisoned us and to the people of Stanley. For six months, while the army built itself a camp, two thousand men were billeted on this village of fifteen hundred people. Some families had ten soldiers or more sleeping in their tiny homes. In the cinema and the Town Hall they slept in rows. In all that time I only had one complaint against a soldier, and that was laid by the village simpleton. Afterwards, when the camp was built and the soldiers had moved out of town, they all made a habit of returning to eat every Sunday dinner with their former hosts. They also provided several husbands for the island girls, much to the fury of our own young men, many of whom were away in the Defence Force, manning coastal batteries.

In this military atmosphere I lost no time in confessing that I had commanded a unit of the Northern Rhodesian Defence Force in Lusaka and had, in my time, made many a gallant and dusty sortie across the airport against no enemy. So now I immediately found myself commanding the infantry company of the Falkland Islands Defence Force instead. This Force was no war-time creation. It had been in existence for about a hundred years. We had an artillery section which spent five years patiently manning the coastal batteries waiting for an enemy ship which never came, and the infantry company. Very sensibly, in such a trackless and boggy wilderness, there were also cavalry units out on the ranches designed to harass the invader.

The islanders are remarkable shots. In Northern Rhodesia, with all my years of hunting, I considered myself quite good with a rifle, but I was not in the same class as the Falkland Islanders. They had the eyes of hawks and were used to shooting on a range in a cross-wind blowing at forty knots. They had collected many trophies at Bisley.

We exercised with the garrison, stalking each other over the peat-bogs in the dark. Soon we were throwing hand grenades and carrying out dashing attacks with live ammunition. But no Japs came and eventually the garrison left to take part in VE Day. Meantime, as in any other Home Guard unit, we got to know one another and to make friends.

After six months I sent for the family. We hated being separated and educating the sons did not, after all, seem to be an insoluble problem. We organized a small posse of teachers to get the elder boy his School Certificate. My wife taught him English and history, the parson taught him geography and scripture, the Government naturalist taught him biology, the Director of Agriculture taught him botany, a corporal in the R.E.M.E. taught him maths and I tried to teach him French and Latin. It was a triumph for him and all of us when, before he sailed to join the Navy, he had his Certificate with three credits. My younger boy, aged ten, fought his way up through the village school. He spent all his spare time, more usefully, 'mucking about in boats'. All my own spare time was taken up with gardening, for unless I grew all the potatoes and all the vegetables for our household of six, there would not have been any.

A remarkable feature of the Falklands was its germ-free soil. It was all peat and in it we could grow the most magnificent vegetables I have ever seen. They said that corpses buried in it did not rot, but I never dug one up to see. In our conservatory in the summer-time the brilliant sun drew our flowers up to fantastic legginess. It was difficult to recognize a snapdragon when it stood four feet tall and its bloom spread thinly down twelve inches or more from the top of the stem.

So I added schoolmastering and horticulture to my amateur repertoire, and I also learned more about the techniques of government because even in that tiny community we had the whole paraphernalia of colonial government to work our parish pump. We had a Civil Service, a High Court and Departments, as well as a little Parliament and an Executive Council. I learned how to draw up a Budget, how to pilot Bills through a Legislature (of sorts) and how to run a little Civil Service, techniques which were to prove valuable to me later on. We, the Honourables, all took ourselves far too seriously, of course, whether we were officials or members of the Legislative Council. That is the trouble with islands and parish pumps. A hierarchy is so ridiculous in miniature. Professor Parkinson would have enjoyed himself in Stanley.

Soon after my arrival we heard that the Argentine intended to annexe Grahamland and the islands round that part of the Antarctic coast. They had formed part of the Falkland Island Dependencies ever since Britain had annexed them in 1908. In years gone by we had kept a magistrate down there in the ice and snow to supervise a big shore whaling station on Deception Island, but, shortly before the war, with the change-over to pelagic whaling operated from factory ships at sea, the shore station had been closed and the Dependencies had become once more uninhabited.

K

The Colonial Office now decided that they must be occupied again, and an expedition was sent out called Operation Tabarin, to establish bases for meteorological and scientific research. This operation was the forerunner of the famous Falkland Islands Dependencies Survey,[1] which has been working in British Antarctica ever since. Stanley became the forward link for maintaining the bases set up in the Antarctic and we became responsible for procuring their supplies. A great deal of my time, in consequence, was spent in checking long lists of stores ordered by radio from Grahamland and in trying to procure them locally, or in South America or in London. This was not easy in the middle of the war as the needs of our explorers included almost every common necessity of life, as well as a great many other things which were highly specialized, such as pemmican and a particular type of petrol container which had been used by Rommel's troops in North Africa. So I learned, too, how to run a general store and a mail order service, and the vital importance of always, somehow, from somewhere, procuring exactly what had been asked for. The wrong kind of wireless valve or cotton instead of thread to sew up a torn *parka* might well mean death to men out with sledges on the icecap. I had learned this lesson on the very day when the expedition's ship had docked at Stanley on her way south. Somewhere, someone had broached the cases of brandy and stolen half the carefully calculated supply. Every member of the expedition had murder in his heart that day. Luckily, we had plenty more for them in our warehouses.

When the relief ship arrived in the following summer, my elder son and I were allowed to go down to the Antarctic 'just for the ride'. Some additional bases had to be set up, so we took the *Fitzroy* down as well, and in her I spent some of the most exciting weeks of my whole life in a strange and splendid world.

I remember standing on the reeling deck in a typical westerly south-east of the Horn when a great sailing ship scudded across our bows like a ghost. The man standing next to me cried out, 'The *Lawhill*! I sailed in her before the war. . . .' She was running down her easting, perhaps loaded with wheat from Australia for

[1] Now called the British Antarctic Dependencies Survey.

South Africa, riding before the western winds half-way across the world.

I remember the first iceberg we met, rising in a tall grey pyramid out of the low-lying fog. In the centre of it, half-way up, there was a pale-blue cave, and in the cave was a shaft of gold, pierced downward into the heart of the berg by the sun we could not see.

Next morning we were in another world. We had left the open, gale-torn sea and were cruising through the islands. The sun was high in a cloudless sky and the sea was calm, like pale-blue watered silk. Out of it the islands and the distant coast of Grahamland rose above black cliffs into golden-tinted snowfields and cold, sunlit peaks. The still water around us was, when I looked straight down into it, black as mud, so thick it was with plankton. In it were millions of little translucent, pink, shrimp-like creatures. These were the krill which feeds on the plankton, and feeding on the krill was almost every other creature that lives in the Antarctic. Petrels, great and small, skua and rose-breasted gulls wheeled and skimmed about us; dolphins, seals and penguins broke surface everywhere; and under a dark cliff whales were spouting.

Later I saw ten terrible killer-whales hunting in a pack. Each of them was twenty feet or more in length and they came past us very close, black on top and white beneath, their long vicious jaws bristling with teeth, and their great dorsal fins slicing through the surface like black knives. They hunt anything and everything, and will even dive beneath the ice and thrust it upwards to dislodge a seal basking in the sun, or a man fishing through a hole.

These and many other marvels filled my days. They have all been described many times in books by men who really know the Antarctic. As a mere tourist, I would not presume upon their company, except, perhaps, to tell of two little private adventures of my own.

One afternoon in December, having nosed our way through the ice down the long Neumeyer Channel between avalanche-thundering mountains, we came to a base called Port Lockroy.

We had with us men sent down to relieve those who had been there for a year. That evening we all sat down to an enormous meal and a hilarious amount of drink. Later I wandered off down the passage of the very commodious hut and found myself standing in a little room which contained not only a porcelain bath, but also a porcelain lavatory with a plug that pulled. Standing there, amid all this shining luxury, I suddenly realized that I was, at that ridiculous moment, the southernmost man in the whole world.

Through a little window I could see the top of a small perfect, snow-clad mountain, shining, pink as a sugar-coated almond, in its own little private alpenglow, but even as I watched a great black cloud swept over it, and all the world between was filled with snow, and a shrieking, icy wind. This is how the Antarctic always behaves. For a few hours, or a few days in summer-time, the sun shines and all the beauty with it (that is when the photographs are taken and when Dr. Wilson painted his pictures). Then, suddenly, perhaps for days on end, a raging blizzard screams down from the polar plateau with death in its wings. As I stood there, however undignified, and watched it come, I thought of Scott and Shackleton and Cherry Garrard on their terrible journeys, and suddenly felt that the Antarctic was a place to make any Englishman proud. Years later I was to feel this again, in the Khyber Pass, when from the comfort of a modern limousine I saw the crests of British regiments carved upon the hills, where they had stood guard over the back door to India for more than a hundred years.

My only personal contribution to Antarctic history was almost equally ridiculous. We wanted to build a hut in the South Orkney Islands to be occupied in the following season, and I was allowed to take the *Fitzroy* and do it. In order to get there, we had to thread our way through more than a thousand flat-topped ice-bergs. It was like passing through the streets of a city built of green, blue and silver glass. The captain, like a traffic cop, was ordering the man at the wheel to 'take the second turning on the left', or 'the first on the right', as the case might be. Unfortunately, as we entered the bay for which we were bound, a gale sprang up and we had no time to do more than pile the pieces of the hut on shore and run for the open sea before the icebergs blocked the entrance. Also unfortunately, about a million penguins were nesting on the shore and the ground was inches deep in filth. The smell made some of us very sick. I have often wondered if anybody ever found our piled-up hut or put it together and lived in it.

The Colonial Office had told me that my appointment in the Falklands would be for only three years, and in July 1945 I was offered the post of Under Secretary in the Gold Coast. This was a surprise because the Gold Coast, still eleven years from becoming independent Ghana, was the most highly developed and prosperous colony in tropical Africa. As Under Secretary I should have to act as Colonial Secretary for much of the time, when either the Governor or the Colonial Secretary himself was on leave. It was going to be a formidable jump from my tiny office in Stanley.

The offer was, however, a great relief. At last we would be able to get our younger boy to school in England. The elder was soon to leave us to go home on a cargo ship to join the Navy. Unfortunately, the Governor of the Falklands, who had never been well, was now so ill that we ourselves had to put off going until we heard that my successor had been appointed and was on his way out. We could not leave until November and, as I was due in Accra in February, we should have to go without most of the six months' leave that was due to us. As it turned out, we had only six weeks at home because we had to wait for two months in Uruguay for a ship to sail from Montevideo. Eventually, we managed to get passages on a meat-ship and meanwhile we had had a lovely summer holiday on the estuary of the River Plate which did us much more good than an English winter. We spent some of it down-river at Atlantida, lying under hot, scented pines or bathing, and some of it at Pocitos, a much more sophisticated resort near Montevideo, where cohorts of young Uruguayans did physical exercises on the beach before breakfast. Here we moved briefly into the unfamiliar diplomatic world and were invited to so many cocktail parties that we wondered whether cirrhosis of the liver might not be an occupational disease of the Foreign Service.

It was a strange and cheerful interlude which served very well to reduce the Falklands to their proper perspective. After a while we felt less like lost sheep and hoped that we did not look like them. We stopped being parish-pump bores about our islands and when a relief ship for the Dependencies came into port our last contact with the Antarctic turned out to be in merry keeping with my other memories of it. Some of the huskies on board broke loose and created howling mayhem in the docks.

CHAPTER 12

West Africa

WE arrived in England in the New Year and after six weeks I left my wife in Oxford to settle the school problem and flew out to Accra. I travelled in a rickety Dakota which went all round the bulge of Africa, hugging the coast in case it had to make a forced landing on the beach, between the roaring surf and the edge, first of the desert and then of the interminable forest.

At the airport in the Gambia the first shock was waiting for me in the person of Sir Henry Gurney. He was then Colonial Secretary of the Gold Coast, and more than anything I had looked forward to having him as my chief. He had been in East Africa for many years and everywhere in the Service he was much loved and admired. He just had time before his plane left to tell me that he was on his way home on leave.

'Who is acting Colonial Secretary?' I asked.

'You are', he said.

Then he laughed and added, 'Don't worry. You have a splendid Governor and a Rolls-Royce Secretariat to help you.'

He smiled, winked one hooded eye and vanished through the door.

Gurney came back to Accra three months later to act as Governor. Then he went off to Palestine to be High Commissioner, a thankless task if ever there was one, and after that to Malaya, where he was ambushed by Communist guerrillas and murdered. Characteristically, he had taken too little thought for his own safety. It was a sad and bitter waste of one of the finest men in the Colonial Service.

To come to the Gold Coast after Northern Rhodesia was, in terms of western civilization, to jump forward three generations in time and, once more, into a totally different world. Here was a small, compact country, inhabited by handsome, alert, vigorous

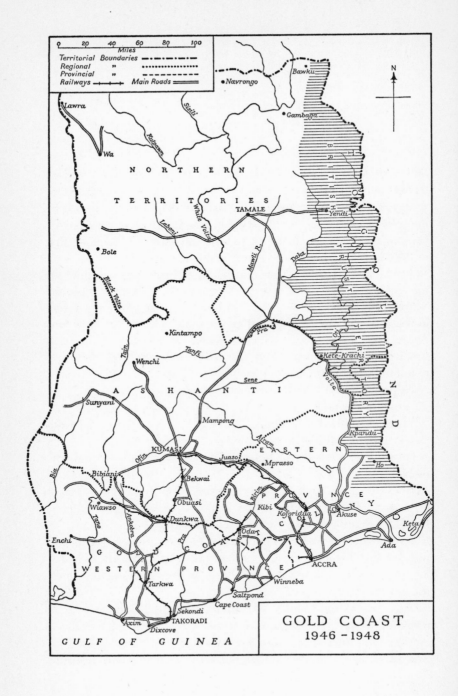

GOLD COAST
1946 - 1948

and intelligent people who had grown prosperous, by African standards, on the export of cocoa, gold, diamonds and timbers. The coastal peoples had been in touch with Europe for five hundred years. In the inland forests the Ashanti had a highly developed Negro kingdom which, unlike Benin, was not already decadent when the Europeans came. Only the Northern Territories, lying between the forest and the desert, were still as primitive as the Africa I had known.

Here, near the coast, were African cities with big secondary boarding-schools for boys and girls. Here was Achimota, the most famous school in tropical Africa; here were African judges, barristers, doctors, business men, and a numerous middle class of prosperous sophisticated people; here were Chiefs who wore great ornaments of gold and walked under huge state umbrellas to their chauffeur-driven cars; here were cathedrals and churches and a public library. Here, too, was witchcraft as foul as the slime of the mangrove swamps where it had been bred, and in the dark forests, it seemed, dwelt spirits far more sinister than those of the sunny woodlands of Central Africa. Men lived in fear of them and found release from it in quick laughter and sudden, hot-tempered violence.

On my very first morning in the office the telephone rang.

'This is the Commissioner of Police. I just want to report a battle. Two villages up the road. A hundred a side. Cutlasses mostly. No dead. I sent out a truckload of police. No casualties.'

'Tell me', I said, very much astonished, 'does this kind of thing often happen here?'

'Yes', he said, 'every Sunday afternoon.'

'What about the D.C.?'

'Oh, they just form a ring round him to keep him safe and carry on.'

I went to my first meeting of the Executive Council and there I found that the leading African politicians who were members of it were quicker-witted than I and just as highly educated. I do not easily quote Browning in Council meetings. I had never met Africans like this before, and I looked forward to trying to make friends with them and to having them as colleagues.

I was also looking forward to working with the Governor, Sir Alan Burns, who was a shrewd, fearless administrator, a Scot, born and brought up in the West Indies. 'The secret of good administration', he once told me, 'is always to be one jump ahead of the people. Give them what they want before they know they want it.' Only a few days later an African politician put it to us this way: 'Never tell our people they must learn to walk before they can run. Let us run and pick ourselves up when we fall down.' No wonder they liked and admired Sir Alan. He certainly followed the African's advice with me, because I had hardly unpacked before he was away on a three weeks' tour up-country and left me to run on my own.

Gurney had been right about the Secretariat. It was large and competent and full of expertise. This was fortunate for me because so many of the files which passed across my desk dealt with matters like exchange control, cocoa marketing and other problems of a complex, developed economy which had never arisen in the simplicities of Central Africa or the Falklands. There was only one thing to do and that was to follow the advice of another famous Governor. This one had said, 'The essence of good administration is to delegate responsibility. Leave men free to use their own judgment, but insist on full reporting so that you know what they are doing.'

So I let the experts and bright young men get on with it, which saved us all a lot of work and me, I hope, from making too many mistakes. It also gave me time to get to know something about the country and its people, and time to think. As I had learned in Lusaka, nobody can *think* if he spends ten hours a day battling against a flood of files.

That was an exciting year of exploration and adventure. It was a revelation, when Empire Day came round, to see the African schoolchildren of Accra parading on the polo ground, marching past, thousands of them, rank after rank, in smart school uniforms. It was a moving experience to watch the students at Achimota perform *The Barretts of Wimpole Street*. My wife ventured to ask an African lady who was sitting next to her why such a very English play, so Victorian and to us so distasteful, should have been chosen. Her friend laughed and replied, 'Old Mr. Barrett? My grandfather was just like him!' It was not difficult to imagine the old gentleman. Only the other day I had myself seen just such a one. He, in grey top hat and morning coat, and his lady in flowered hat and gloves, had been conducting their family, walking two by two, to matins in the cathedral.

We heard Handel's *Messiah* splendidly sung by the local choral society with Europeans and Africans in both chorus and orchestra. It was fun to go to a ball at Cape Coast, where all the African men wore brilliant *kente* cloths and all the girls long, sophisticated evening gowns. We danced to a band which may have since made itself rich in the night clubs of the world.

It was fun, too, to have picnics on a beach some ten miles down the coast where the village headman had allowed us to build a shelter. We had sealed the bargain with a bottle of gin, as was the custom of the country, and had together poured a libation to the gods.

Best of all, perhaps, was the day when the Asantehene, the Paramount Chief of the Ashanti, came down to Accra in state and progressed through the city with five thousand followers, under a bobbing line of huge, coloured umbrellas to the beat of drums and the deep blasts of horns made from elephant tusks. The Asantehene, himself, whom I had last met at a dinner party in a dinner jacket, wore splendid robes and was so heavily weighed down with gold that two boys had to support him as he walked along bowing to us all.

If one had come out to Accra with no previous experience of Africa and with no preconceived ideas about Africans, one would have been astonished not so much by the complex and highly developed culture of the people as by their apparent ability to graft on to it so much of an alien European civilization without breaking down under the spiritual and psychological conflicts which must have been entailed.

One English postgraduate student came out from London to study for a thesis on this very subject. It was to be written round case-histories of students at Achimota who had had nervous breakdowns as a result of such conflicts. He could not find any and decided to find a different subject for his thesis, though their very absence would itself have given him a fascinating theme.

On me, however, with so many years' experience in Central Africa, the impact of the Gold Coast was, at first, rather different. So many of the pipe-dreams we had had at Fort Jameson for the future of the Angoni and Achewa had here come true. So many of our castles in the air were here already built. It was, of course, obvious that these Negro peoples belonged to a quite different stock from the Bantu of Central Africa, and they seemed to be of higher calibre. Some said this was because they had all been using vitamin-rich palm-oil in their diet for a thousand years, whereas the Central Africans had had to make do with water-melon seeds. Others gave the credit to those strict Victorian grandparents, the Mr. Barretts of Cape Coast and Accra. In any event, these people were no more like the Central Africans than we are like the Eskimos.

We soon learned to love and admire them for their good manners, courtesy, tolerance and sheer good looks. Later we began, of course, to see some weaknesses, which were, I dare say, the heritage of history and environment. We tried not to expect the people to be like ourselves and tried to understand how a totally different code of inherited ethics sometimes operated and why.

Meantime, the Governor was pressing on with the development of parliamentary democracy and I was becoming deeply involved in local politics. It was early in 1947 that Sir Alan Burns anticipated the demands of the then highly respectable nationalist movement by bringing in a new constitution. It gave the elected representatives of the Africans a majority in the Legislative Council and, more important, on the standing Finance Committee which controlled the purse-strings of Government. Although the initiative in legislation still lay with the Governor and although he still retained power to veto any irresponsible action by the legislature, government ceased to be imposed and was carried on by consultation. Except in an emergency, nothing would or could be done unless the Africans agreed with it. This was the last stage in political training before responsibility would be devolved on to elected African Ministers, which would, in turn, lead to full self-government. No other European dependency in Africa, not even Nigeria, had come nearly so far along the road to independence. The introduction of the Burns constitution was welcomed by the people with great pride. At that particular stage, the Gold Coast was, politically and for the moment, a mutual admiration society. We were *all* nationalists and proud of it.

It fell to me to act as Leader of the House in that session of the Legislative Council when officials were for the first time in a small minority and no longer in control. There were only six of us in a Council of thirty-six members. By coincidence we all came in one day with red roses in our buttonholes. They did not symbolize red rebellion, but were purely frivolous.

Few Colonial Service officials enjoyed playing politics or were very good at it. They disliked the log-rolling, lobbying and intrigue which seemed to be involved. As Civil Servants and administrators we had been brought up to eschew politics altogether, and few of us could change our spots with any pleasure or success. I, for one, was a deplorable parliamentarian.

This was, perhaps, a weakness in me or in the system, but I cannot believe that trained British politicians imported for the purpose would have been any more successful. They have seldom made good Governors. We, at least, tried to know the people and the economic and social needs of the country, which is what politics are all about, or should be.

Personally, I was no more convinced then than I had been in Northern Rhodesia, or than I am today, that the introduction of western-type democracy into African society makes men and women happier. We had no alternative. We were, quite rightly, fully committed to training the people for self-government and we could only teach them what we knew. The Africans themselves in every British colony were demanding the 'Westminster model' and would not have accepted anything else. I remember Sir James Coussey, the African judge, who was asked to recommend a constitution for an independent Ghana, confirming this. He had, with a lawyer's capacity for taking pains, read through every written constitution in the world, asking himself what Ghana needed, and what Ghanaians would accept. It had, in the end, to be the 'Westminster model', and only later did they begin to experiment with a one-party state and other adaptations perhaps better suited to their needs. The remarkable thing is not that some of the new countries seem to have moved away from the Mother of Parliaments, but that so many of them are still trying to copy her.

Unfortunately, the political honeymoon of mutual admiration in the Gold Coast did not last for very long. Sir Alan Burns retired, Dr. Kwame Nkrumah arrived, and within a very few months the country was in a revolutionary turmoil.

I have written here about the short-lived Burns constitution partly because the experience which my small part in it gave me taught me sympathy with nationalism in colonial affairs, and partly because none of the many books and treatises which have since been written about Ghana seem to me to have given it sufficient importance. In the context of Africa nearly twenty years ago, it was a bold and friendly experiment which gives the lie to so much that is now believed about the 'dead hand' of British colonialism. 'Freedom' has become a cliché. Freedom from what? In Northern Rhodesia, fifty years earlier, the people had wanted freedom, too, freedom from the Arab slave-traders and from the tyranny of the warrior-tribes. They had asked us for it and we had given it to them, and they were, for a generation or so, content. Nationalism and the conviction that political independence is a self-evident right came only with the spread of education. In the Gold Coast, and later in all our African colonies, we had, rather belatedly, come to realize that this would be so, but we did not do so grudgingly. On the contrary, we all became, in varying degrees, good nationalists. There was no difference of principle between the British and Nkrumah. The only question was, how soon? All that we can say, with the gift of hindsight, is that we were still handing out democracy in doses as big as we thought the Africans could take instead of giving them the bottle; or, to revert to a previous metaphor, in our grandmotherly way were still trying to teach the people to walk before letting them run. The lessons of the long nationalist struggle in India, which was just then leading up to the partition of the sub-continent, had not penetrated more deeply than that into our official thinking in West Africa. It was Nkrumah who, with sharper vision, taught his people, and especially the eager young men, that they should demand to be allowed to run and pick themselves up when they fell down. In no time at all he swept them off their feet. He upset the whole process of political evolution in Ghana, and by his example speeded it up throughout tropical Africa.

But I am not going to write about that, because so much has been written already, and indeed the story of Nkrumah is still unfolding.

We went on a very short leave in the summer of 1947 and when I came back the atmosphere of the country had already changed, so swiftly did Nkrumah move. The boil of political discontent burst in February 1948 in the form of large-scale, organized rioting in Accra and other places.

Those riots are seldom mentioned nowadays. They have been overlaid by so many other tragedies of violence all over the world, but for three days we did have great mobs in the streets, looting and burning in a wild orgy of anarchy and greed. It was the first time anything like this had happened in British Africa. For all of us it was a terrible experience and the more so that it could have happened in the Gold Coast, the model dependency on which so many hopes were founded. It was a horrid experience, too, for so many of our African friends, who were frightened and bitterly ashamed, and whom we could not help, for we might compromise them by our very friendship.

'Civil disturbance', when used to describe anything more than a rowdy meeting, is a masterpiece of official understatement, as anyone knows who has heard the howling of a mob. For those three days in Accra we heard it, with 50,000 people in the streets. The veneer of civilization seemed to have been stripped off and what lay underneath looked very ugly.

The more extreme nationalists who organized the rebellion, for that is what it was, were not anti-European or even anti-British, they were just pro-African, for Africans are seldom racialists unless they are driven to it by bitter personal experience and the colour bar, or by despair in the face of a stubborn refusal to grant them dignity.[1] There were one or two nationalist leaders in the Gold Coast who had been embittered in this way at some time in their lives, but there was no social or economic gulf between Europeans and Africans. On the whole, we liked and respected each other. Many of us were close friends. Yet once the revolutionary technique of inflaming the masses is embarked upon, in any country where two races live, pride of race is invoked and hatred is also sparked into flame. This happened in Accra, but not for long. Within a week our wives could go shopping again in the market with their African friends and meet only the old cheerful smiles. No Europeans were killed during the whole affair, and as far as we knew (which was by no means all) only about twenty rioters. Considering the size of the mobs, the casualties were remarkably few.

The purpose of the nationalist leaders was purely political, to force the British Government to grant self-government to the Gold Coast at once, instead of by stages. They did not believe that the British would ever give it to them of their own accord, in spite of the Burns constitution and in spite of repeated declarations that self-government was the goal. They chose their moment well. The post-war inflation had led to a sharp rise in prices, which had in turn resulted in a complete boycott of all imported consumer goods. This had been so effective that the people had realized the power they could exercise when they were well led and organized. At the same time there were a few hundred of the thousands of recently demobilized ex-servicemen who did not want to return to their villages to farm, nor to work as labourers. Both the mood of the people and this hard core of disgruntled veterans were ripe for exploitation.

The nationalists achieved independence in 1957, nine years later, and who is to say now whether they would have done so faster or slower by peaceful persuasion? What is certain is that Nkrumah, by his example, let loose the 'wind of change' which was, in less than twenty years, to blow all colonial régimes out of tropical Africa.

[1] This is not disproved by the periodic killing of Europeans in the Congo since 1957. That is savagery, for which some of the Congo tribes have always been notorious.

When the riots started I was already somewhat detached in spirit from the Gold Coast because I had, a few weeks earlier, accepted an offer from the Colonial Office to go and work in London. At that time, both the new Governor and the new Colonial Secretary were in Accra, and I had reverted temporarily to my proper post of Under Secretary. Almost immediately I was seconded to go and take over the Information and Broadcasting Services until the emergency ended. I was promised complete freedom of action, including the right to hand-pick extra staff from the Administration. For once I was told not to count the cost. So, with alacrity, I exchanged the collar and tie of bureacracy for an open shirt and what came to be known in the Information Department as 'Bradley's fighting shorts'. They were made of a rather bright-blue linen and were very short. We went into action.

We launched a daily news-sheet, lengthened the broadcasting programmes, showered the local newspapers with hand-outs and dealt with a not very large influx of overseas journalists. Our policy was quite simple. The reaction from the violence and chaos of the first three days was already setting in and we knew that the great majority of the people would be suffering from shock. Most of the listeners to the radio were town-dwellers of the artisan, professional and commercial classes and most of them were Christians. The spiritual and civic values by which they lived had been submerged in a horrifying wave of savage anarchy, and they were, for the moment, bewildered and lost. So we gave them straightforward Christian ethics and the truth about the emergency as we understood it. We tried to be positive and we did not argue. This policy and, especially, the daily news-sheet, which was given a very big free circulation, were most unpopular with the extremists, who sent us dire threats of assassination, but it probably had a stabilizing effect and did something to speed up a return to normality.

The memories which stand out most clearly from the confusion of those dark days are those of the loyalty and courage shown by so many individual Ghanaians, and of the generosity with which many Europeans and Africans resealed old friendships as soon as ever this became possible.

By the time we sailed for England, three months later, everyone was more concerned with what the inevitable Commission of Inquiry would recommend, than with troubles which had given rise to it. Mercifully the Ghanaians are always much more interested in the future than in the past, for their world is young and they have been leading Africa into it.

It was sad that my last few months in the Colonial Service should have been spent in circumstances which were in such shocking contrast to the twenty-two years before them. Yet now I am grateful for those two years in Accra not only for the memories of happy days and many friends but because the riots helped me to understand both the nature of nationalism and the problems which usually arise during the last few difficult years before a colony becomes independent. If I had left the Service twelve months earlier, with untarnished memories of the golden years, I would, I expect, have found it very hard to adjust my thinking to the realities of Asia and Africa during the next fifteen years, or to do much of the work which I have been doing since 1948.

However, memory is kind and when I think back now to those Gold Coast days my most frequent recollections are not of mobs or politics or even the sweat and sleepless discomfort of those hot, breathless nights. I remember other things so much more vividly.

Every Sunday we spent on the beach riding in on the great, warm, tumbling surf, watching the fishing canoes come in with their tawny, triangular sails bright against the hot sky, and mingling with the cheerful crowd of women and children waiting to buy the catch. In our palm-thatched shelter we played hilarious games of 'liar-dice' on a blanket, ate splendid curries and slept them off in the cool sea-breeze.

Most vividly I remember riding in on the surf one moonlit night when our wave sparkled as it moved, like a diamond necklace, and the feathery crowns of the coconut palms stood, in rare stillness, a black frieze against the sky. I remember, too, the scarlet blossoms of the creeper called 'Ashanti blood' shining in the dark forest, and the grey trunks of the silk-cotton trees rising like thin pencils, two hundred feet tall, against the blue hills.

I like to think of the fun we had, a dozen Africans and I, when we were turned into a Commission by Sir Alan Burns to go round the country and find out whether the people wanted a university of their own or would prefer to send their sons and daughters to a bigger university for the whole of West Africa to be built in Nigeria. Like Scotsmen, they had no doubts whatever on such a subject. We ended our Inquiry on the top of Lagon Hill outside Accra and said very firmly that we should have our own university and that it should be built on that breezy hill-top not far from Achimota with all its fine traditions. And so it was.

I remember when we had the railways and the gold-mines out on strike all at once for several weeks, a strike so well and so cheerfully organized that there was not a single incident and not one of the 50,000 strikers had to be arrested. In the end it was the African members of the Legislative Council who persuaded the railway union to send its men back to work. When I told them that they had made history, for who had ever heard of back-bench M.P.s anywhere settling a strike in a national industry, let alone in Africa, they looked rather surprised and answered, 'But we always make history in the Gold Coast'. They are still making it.

I am glad that, during those few weeks at the very end of my service, I had a chance to take my coat off and get back into my old harness as Information Officer. At the end of my Secretariat career I was no happier in it than I ever had been and not, I think, very much more skilful. I enjoyed negotiation and trying to bring a little humanity into a rather inhuman bureaucracy, but I hated political intrigue and disputation and files and precedents. In any case I had long ago learned that I was more effective when paddling my own canoe, however small, than in working up to someone else. I was never a very good Number Two.

On the whole, then, we were glad to go. My wife and I were tired of being members of that social hierarchy based on official position which was the curse of British colonial society. We had had a good many months at the top when either the Governor or the Colonial Secretary had been on leave. My wife said she had felt like a Victorian wax posy under a glass dome. As for me I never wanted to work again in any hierarchy of any sort.

CHAPTER 13

Corona

THE Colonial Office wanted me to come home and start a professional journal for the Colonial Service. Since 1946 thousands of recruits had been pouring into the Service to fill the war-time gaps and to help to carry out long-delayed programmes of economic and social development. The Service was larger than it had ever been and relatively inexperienced. It included an ever-growing variety of specialists and it was scattered right round the world. It needed its own journal to give its members a greater sense of unity and to provide a means through which men dealing with similar problems in different territories could exchange experiences and ideas. It seemed, however, that I would have to retire, at the age of only forty-five, because I would need a pension to supplement the meagre salary which was all the Colonial Office could afford to pay an editor.

Here was a poser indeed. Was I to retire just when things looked so promising? But were they so promising for me? Still something of a misfit in a Secretariat, would I be given promotion and even if I were, did I really want to be a Colonial Secretary in a big colony immersed in politics and files? On the other hand, did I want to retire at forty-five, ten years before I need, into what might be a dead-end job, even though it might last me till I was sixty-five? Yet the challenge of starting such a useful and badly needed journal was attractive. So, indeed, was the prospect of being able to spend the rest of my life with writing and writers, giving others a magazine in which they could help each other professionally, let off steam — or poetry — and teach themselves to write, as I had once tried to do.

In the end these questions seemed to both of us less important than the fact that our two boys would be needing us at home while they were finishing their much-interrupted education and facing the problems of careers. Twice before their interests had been sacrificed, on the outbreak of war, and when we went to the Falklands. Here was a chance to prevent that happening again. So I said 'yes' and in June 1948 we sailed for England, ready once again to start a new life. Post-war England would, after all these years, be very strange to us.

We set up house in London and we have lived there ever since. It was difficult at the start, partly because we had not been there during the war to share the hardships and dangers which everybody else had endured. We felt like interlopers. Living, too, was difficult for everyone in those ration-ridden days. Always before, at home and abroad, there had been domestic servants and now there were none. The much-advertised social revolution, in terms of the breakdown of class and privilege, did not dismay us, in spite of the fact that we had, for nearly twenty-five years, belonged to a privileged ruling class in colonial society. We had spent all our most impressionable years in Rhodesia where the strong pioneering tradition mocked at privilege and social distinctions, and where men and women were, on the whole, judged on their merits. We had found the nineteenth-century social outlook of the Falklands, with its squirearchy of ranchers exercising almost feudal rights over the workers, distasteful, and we had disliked even more, because we were involved in it, the petty official snobberies of the Gold Coast. Strangers or not, we felt much more at home in post-war England, and were delighted by the kindness and the respect, amounting almost to affection, with which Londoners seemed to treat each other. They had been through so much together.

'Isn't it true', said an American friend to us, 'that in this country you have abolished poverty as a social problem?' The reason why that remark has stayed in my memory is that at the time it made me feel proud of the way in which our people were carrying out their revolution and did much to reconcile me to the taxation and inflation which between them were lowering the value of my poor little pension.

Nevertheless we did not find it easy to learn to live in London. We had been abroad almost continuously for twenty-two years, we had put down no roots anywhere, and most of our friends were still in Africa. The idea of starting again in a new environment did not daunt us, because we had done it so many times before — in Northern Rhodesia, the Falklands and West Africa. What we had not realized was the totally different way of living involved in a 'nine to five' professional job in London. Ever since that agricultural show which we had both so enjoyed arranging at Fort Jameson in 1927, right through the years to those last tragic weeks in Accra, my wife had always shared in my work, whether on *ulendo* together in the bush, or making gardens, or doctoring African babies or arguing with me about Chiefs and roads and policies. Perforce our friends had been my colleagues and their wives, and conversation round our dinner table had always been unashamedly shop. The work *was* our lives. But England, and especially London, is not like that. Colleagues are rarely the friends you meet at home, for they live scattered in the great city or more probably in the suburbs and Home Counties. Nor, it seemed, could my wife and I any longer share my work because it was just as detached from our home as it would have been if I had been a chartered accountant.

We have discussed this problem with many others who have returned from the uttermost parts of the earth, and they all seem to agree that the problems of educating your children while you are abroad and of making the difficult adjustment to life in England when you retire are the two chief drawbacks to working overseas.

I spent rather more than four years editing our new Colonial Service journal. The Colonial Office was, from the start, as helpful as could be. They gave me a set of offices, an assistant editor for as long as I needed one to get the journal launched, and a secretary. They also told me that I could have complete freedom of action and, most definitely, was not a member of the office hierarchy. This was admirable. The only difficulty was that I had never, even in Lusaka, learned very much about the techniques of magazine production and of printing as distinct from editing. So to this extent I was once again the amateur as I had so often been in so many jobs for all those twenty-two years.

The wife of an absent District Officer came to help as assistant editor, just as those other wives had once helped in Lusaka. I can still see us crawling about the floor of the office at nine in the evening, with pins in our mouths and scissors in hand, struggling to make up the galley proofs of our first number into pages. None of the articles would fit, we hated to sacrifice a line of them and the printers were waiting. The other techniques were not so difficult and we managed to produce that first monthly issue in February 1949, four months after we had set up the office. It only contained one bad howler.

The most difficult problem, really, was to find a name for the journal. We eventually chose *Corona* because the Crown was the obvious unifying symbol of His Majesty's Colonial Service. Nobody liked the name any more than we did but, even though it did make everybody think of cigars and soft drinks, nobody could think of a better one.

Circulation was no problem because the Colonial Office told everyone in the Service about *Corona* and it was welcomed. Nor did we have to wait very long for material. There were, it seemed, a surprising number of would-be writers, artists and poets scattered in far-flung outposts from the West Indies to the Pacific. Manuscripts soon began to come in.

At that time the transformation of the Empire into the new multi-racial Commonwealth had only just started, with the independence of India and Pakistan in 1947, closely followed by Ceylon in 1948. Burma had gone, Malaya was fighting her Communists, and all the other dependencies were at varying stages of political and social emancipation, ranging from the first tentative introduction of local authorities in the primitive and war-ravaged Solomon Islands to the last delicate stages which had just been so impatiently upset in the Gold Coast.

The policy was to give independence in due course to any dependency which asked for it when, in the opinion of the British Government, its people were capable of standing on their own feet in a highly competitive and unscrupulous world. The country must be able to balance its budget and to command enough confidence to attract capital for development; its peoples must be sufficiently united to guarantee political stability, and there must be enough educated men and women to man its Civil Service and the professions and to play a responsible role in industry and commerce. If any colony were to be given independence before these conditions had been fulfilled we should, it was said, have betrayed our trust.

The corollaries of this long-term policy were not only that there should be enough money made available to colonial governments for the necessary economic and educational development, but also that the new nationalist movements should not be suppressed but guided into constructive co-operation. The Colonial Development and Welfare Act, passed as a noble gesture in the darkest days of 1940, had belatedly revised the old system by which every colony had been expected to pay its own way, and could only get capital grants from Britain for development projects which would be revenue-earning. By now, every dependency had its own five- or ten-year development plan. Those which were poor could draw heavily on the 'C.D. & W.' grants, those which were rich, like the Gold Coast, could not get so much. The British taxpayer, of course, could never be expected to produce all the money which would be needed, and it was therefore all the more necessary that the colonies should move towards independence peacefully and in good order, building up their economies as they went. Otherwise they would not be able to attract private investment for their future capital development after independence, and then where would they be?

This, in 1950, seemed to be a sensible and honourable policy, so far as it went and, as the importance of helping the under-developed countries came to be accepted by the United States and the whole elaborate system of international aid began to grow, it looked more practicable. It even survived the outrageous fiasco of Tanganyika's groundnut scheme, on which £30 millions were wasted, millions which could have been used to give the whole of East Africa the education system it so badly needed.

Unfortunately, *time* was needed, decades of time, and this was not to be vouchsafed. It was not to be expected that the Colonial

Office — after a hundred years or more of *Pax Britannica* — could foresee the force and urgency of the nationalism which was sparked off in Africa by Nkrumah. The new Commonwealth was already in existence. Ghana and Nigeria would no doubt join it before very long, but as for East and Central Africa, was not the pace of Africa still the pace of the ox?

The surprising thing, looking back from 1965, is not the degree to which those principles of post-war British policy have inevitably weakened under the irresistible pressures of nationalism, but that the whole process of de-colonization, however hurried it has had to be, has been so peaceful that nearly all the newly independent countries have so far remained politically stable.

In 1950, then, the orderly advance of the colonies to independence seemed to us to be reasonably assured, in spite of Accra. The interest of the Colonial Service was centred less on political questions than on the exciting possibilities of economic and social development, on the spread of higher education and on such new techniques as Community Development. Great efforts were being made everywhere to help and encourage the colonial peoples to join in this drive for their own development. The successful achievement of independence was to be a co-operative effort, whatever the set-backs might be and whatever the critics of colonialism may now say to the contrary.

Corona soon settled into a pattern which it was to retain for the whole of its life. We were never really satisfied with it because there always seemed to be too much material of the house-magazine type — domestic news about Service matters, literary sketches, verse and drawings — and not enough technical articles of the high quality needed to give it standing as a professional journal.

There were two reasons for this: first, our would-be contributors, being Civil Servants, were required by the regulations to submit such technical manuscripts to their own colonial Governments for approval and few of them felt like doing so. They were reluctant, not so much because they wanted to write about politics or to criticize the policy of their Governments, which they were not allowed to do, as because they simply did not want to risk the bother of getting involved in arguments with the Secretariat. This was understandable. It had been one of the reasons why, in writing the *Diary of a District Officer* before the war, I had avoided discussing any administrative problems. The second reason was that members of almost every branch of the Service had access to their own professional journals, ranging from *The Lancet* to *Oversea Education*, which were of more immediate interest to them.

We did, however, get a few good professional articles and as a house journal *Corona* did something to fulfil its purpose. About three thousand members of the Service continued to subscribe half a crown for it during nearly all the fifteen years of its existence. *Corona* came to an end in 1963 because there were so few colonies left that the Service itself was dying.

Long before this, however, by the end of 1952, I had begun to feel that I had had enough of it. I had learned a little about the editor's craft, but not very much because there had never been enough money to be adventurous. Not for us the glamour of glossy paper and coloured illustrations. We had had to make do with a group of photographs in the middle and some line drawings tucked into the text. The most interesting part of the work, and this must be true of all magazine editing, however copious the money bags, had been the discovery of new talent. It was always exciting to open the bulky envelopes plastered with strange stamps from all over the world. They might contain anything from a treatise on the theory of government written by a lonely and thoughtful ex-brigadier now administering a South Sea island, to a poem by a policeman who had fallen under the spell of the desert in the hinterland of Aden. I have often wondered how many of those amateur authors, poets and artists, whose work was first published in *Corona*, were as encouraged as I had been when I read the first instalment of *Mishoro Monty* in the *Wide World* twenty-five years before.

Some of our contributors were very good. Only recently one of them has published a charming book about East Africa and in a national exhibition of Rhodesian art held at the Commonwealth Institute in 1963 I saw a beautiful abstract painting with a familiar signature. It was by a man who had drawn many endearing cartoons for *Corona* while he was still a schoolmaster in Northern Rhodesia, painting in his spare time.

Then, of course, there had been Sir Arthur Grimble and his *Pattern of Islands*. This enchanting book about the South Seas, which brought Grimble fame and fortune after he had retired from the Colonial Service, was born as a series of talks on the B.B.C. I heard the first of them and thought that I had never listened to a more charming story-teller or heard a more beautiful speaking voice. How he had loved his people! I wrote at once to Grimble asking him if he would let us publish them. 'Of course', he said, and we were jubilant. But, alas, he wrote again three days later asking to be released from his promise because the *Reader's Digest* wanted them. We could not compete with that.

We had had our moments, but after five years I saw that *Corona* had set into a mould. It had become static in content and in circu-lation and I could see no way of improving either. It needed a new mind and a new imagination, and I myself badly needed a change.

Then, one morning in the summer of 1952, a piece of paper came on to my desk which said that a new Director for the Imperial Institute would be needed when the present Director retired in February 1953. The Imperial Institute? That was the great Victorian building with the tall tower in Kensington where I had trained for the Colonial Service twenty-seven years before. I had memories of gloomy rooms and echoing exhibition galleries, with stuffed heads on the walls glaring down at wooden show-cases full of things in bottles. What did it do? Between the wars it had been full of scientists who had done very valuable research in minerals and crops and advised colonial governments about them. No place for me — I pushed the paper aside. Then I remembered that all this research work had been taken over by the Colonial Office. What *did* the Institute do? I pulled the paper back again. Apparently it was teaching people about the Commonwealth. This was more like it. People ought to be taught about the Commonwealth, lots more about it. I would like to try that, but no, every retired colonial Governor would apply for a post like this and I would not stand a chance.

On an impulse I picked up the phone and rang someone in the Colonial Office.

'Oh no', he said, 'I wouldn't do that. The Institute is under sentence of death. They are going to pull the building down to make room for extensions to the Imperial College of Science and Technology which lies behind it. You could not save it. You would only get a three-year contract and then you would be on the shelf.'

Close the Institute? It had far too big a job to do. 'I've got a pension', I ventured.

There was a long pause and suddenly the voice at the other end of the telephone came back, 'I say, would you *really* put in for it?'

It was my turn to be cautious.

'It's a big risk. I'll think it over.'

When a man says that he always means that he wants to ask his wife. I did, and she said, 'Do you remember the man in Bulawayo who started that magazine, the *African Observer*, when he was fifty. He told us he had looked at himself in the glass while he was shaving and said, "Life begins at fifty." You're only forty-eight.'

Besides, what had Uncle Henry said?

I do not know whether any ex-Governors did put in for the post, I only saw one other competitor and he was no Governor. My interview by the selection board was almost as short as that which I had had when I was allowed into the Colonial Service.

'What,' they asked me, 'would you do to make the Institute more attractive to the public?'

They had all my experience and qualifications on the papers in front of them and knew all about me. I ventured to be frivolous.

'I would remove the dear old commissionaire at the Inquiry desk and put in a pretty girl.'

Nevertheless, to my surprise, I was offered the directorship, and now it only remained to find someone else to take on *Corona*. This was not difficult, either, and my successor carried on the editorship very successfully for the next ten years.

During my years with *Corona* I had had the opportunity to learn many other things besides the techniques of editing. I had had to make a close and continuous study of colonial affairs and especially of developments in Africa, which were of rapidly growing importance. Armed with the up-to-date, if somewhat superficial knowledge which this study gave me, I had launched out, in 1949, into broadcasting for the B.B.C. and freelance journalism. The techniques of broadcasting and of writing broadcast scripts and articles were not in themselves unfamiliar, for I had not forgotten my days as Information Officer, but the professional standards of Broadcasting House and Fleet Street were very different from those of our amateur efforts in Africa, and I enjoyed trying to add the extra polish which they demanded. I also enjoyed the extra income of several hundred pounds a year which resulted.

Yet I soon found, as I had in Lusaka, that the kind of reporting which I was constantly asked to do by the B.B.C. — the hurried and inevitably slick comment on whatever colonial events or problems happened to be in the news — more and more irritating. The periodical market for feature articles and stories had been steadily shrinking as, one after another, the *Wide World*, *Strand*, *Windsor*, and all the rest of the famous old magazines failed and died. So, in the end, I contented myself with articles for the Central Office of Information which were published in newspapers all over the Commonwealth. This, I thought, was useful and well worth doing, and it was almost the only freelance work which I continued to do after I went to the Institute.

I also began to do some lecturing. I went on a tour to Western Germany, under the auspices of the Foreign Office, and gave a few talks in England to such varied audiences as the Staff College at Camberley, Rotary Clubs, and sixth-form students from grammar schools at one of the first conferences for them organized by my predecessor at the Imperial Institute. These early experiences culminated in 1953 (after I was myself installed at the Institute) in an extensive lecture tour in the United States, sponsored by the Commonwealth Relations Office.

The tours arranged for me in Germany and America seemed at that time to be particularly worthwhile. I felt sorry for my German audiences. Having so recently lost all their own dependencies they could not have much enjoyed hearing how the

British were running theirs, including some that had been German. Yet they were certainly interested. Because they had just emerged from Nazi tyranny and were reacting violently against it and all its myths, they were eager to learn all they could from the outside world. They packed the lecture halls, listened intently, and asked a great many questions. Some were disbelieving, but most of them merely puzzled, because no German had ever thought before of colonies as potentially independent. This was a new idea to be earnestly studied.

My American tour had exactly the opposite purpose. Instead of having to explain that colonial peoples could and should be led into freedom, I had to explain why they were not yet free. For years Americans had been listening to Indians, Irishmen and West African students telling them all about the brutal British imperialists. We had been doing our best to set the record straight, but we were up against the American 'revolutionary tradition' and had not been very successful. Yet there was, after the war, much admiration for the British and I found that most of my listeners were only too pleased to hear and to believe that our colonial policy was not so wicked after all.

Nobody helped me more effectively to convince them of this than the type of African student who rose from the audience to challenge me. Most of these had been in the States for three years or more, drifting from college to college. They did not know what had been happening in Africa, even in their own countries. I could only advise them to go home as soon as they could and give a helping hand.

On this tour I gave forty-nine lectures and broadcasts during a forty-two-day tour, which took me from New York to Georgia and from the Middle West to San Francisco, with a week in Ontario halfway through. It was a wonderful kaleidoscopic experience but in the end an almost insupportable burden. My lectures became like a set of very old gramophone records, which I had to push laboriously round and round because my motor had died on me. But I learned a lot about lecturing and saw a lot of America, and I had one delightful professional experience, the memory of which still makes me laugh.

I was billed to speak in New York with a West African before an audience of some four thousand people. I had been warned that he was going to call his talk 'Africa. The Black Man's Burden — Getting the White Man Out'. I was furious and protested that nothing would induce me to stand up in front of a lot of foreigners and argue with a fellow British subject who was obviously disloyal. I was told, as so often before, to stop arguing and get on with it. The organizers were gleefully waiting for a splendid piece of controversy and they must not be disappointed.

When I met my African fellow-speaker, he greeted my frosty handshake with a little smile and whispered, 'Can you resist pulling the Yankee leg? I can't', and I relaxed. I said my orthodox piece about British colonial policy and it was duly applauded. Then he rose, dressed in splendid robes, and delivered a skilful, witty and constructive little talk on the partnership between his country and mine. As the storm of cheers died down I rose again, ignoring the protest of the disappointed chairman, and shook hands with my fellow-speaker, both of us beaming in mutual good friendship. And that pleased the audience too, though it was not at all what the organizers had expected. I dare say they forgave us.

Showmanship? Of course it was, on both our parts, but then, I suppose, all lecturers, like orators, should have something of the actor in them. From the moment they stand up they have to be acutely sensitive to their audience and all the time they are speaking they must feel themselves joined to their listeners by a hundred threads and must be ready to change their lines or improvise in response to any signal vibrating through them — eyes that stray or close, a ripple of coughing, or, in contrast, laughter stifled for fear of missing something or, and best of all, the utter silence and still faces of the totally absorbed. Good lecturers, like good actors, or writers or artists, are born, not made. The techniques are not difficult to learn, but they alone are not enough. My own particular technical bugbear is to have to lecture from a script. How is one supposed to look down at it and at the same time to be at one with the audience? It is bad enough having to broadcast from a script, to read it as though you are not reading at all but talking with that one special, imagined listener who is supposed to be so essential to the 'me to you' intimacy of the radio. What a relief it was in America to be allowed to broadcast extempore without being tied to the carefully written, rehearsed and pre-timed script on which the B.B.C. in those days always insisted, even in discussion programmes!

The Americans were far ahead of us in this — too far sometimes. In Berkeley, California, no sooner had an English friend and I arrived in the studio to have a discussion on British policy in Africa, than the producer spilt a whole pot of black coffee all down my friend's suit. No sooner had he mopped him up than he said, 'now I want you to listen to what Professor X said on this subject in last week's programme.' The professor had talked rubbish and as he droned along we fumed. Then suddenly the producer, who had been watching both of us and the clock on the wall, said, 'O.K., Bill. I've got the gen'lemen all steamed up. You're on the air.' The combined effect on my friend of a ruined suit and the professor was electric. He burst into furious oratory. I was infected by it and we gave the broadcast of our lives.

If my years with *Corona* did, incidentally, give me a chance to begin to learn some of the techniques of lecturing, I still think perhaps their most useful contribution to the future was that they widened my horizons. For the first time I began to learn about Malaya, the West Indies, the Pacific Islands and other far-away places which, from between my African blinkers, I had never seen or thought about before. By the time I went to the Institute I had at least a superficial knowledge of the whole colonial empire, and very useful it had already been to me in my various activities. But I still knew nothing whatever about the great independent countries of the Commonwealth. I have been learning about them ever since.

CHAPTER 14

The Commonwealth Institute

THE new Commonwealth Institute was opened by the Queen on 6th November 1962. With its gay cluster of flags flying over Kensington High Street, its peaceful lawns and tree-shaded pools, it is now a familiar and accepted feature of the London scene.

Its predecessor, the old Imperial Institute, opened by Queen Victoria in South Kensington in 1893, to which I went in 1953, was just as familiar to an older generation of Londoners. All that is left of it now is its tall central tower, from which still rings out on royal occasions the highest peal of bells in London. The rest of the great building, with its imposing façade designed in Victorian Gothic with oriental overtones, and with a quarter of a mile of exhibition galleries, has been pulled down in order to make room for extensions to the Imperial College of Science and Technology. The old tower, grey and slender, topped by its dome of pale green copper, stands among the rectangular blocks of the scientists like an indestructible Victorian lady embarrassed to find herself in such unsuitable company.

In 1952 the Institute was, as I have said, under sentence of death. It had to be saved.

The challenge was immediate. Unless we could show without delay that it would be possible to realize at least something of the potential of the Institute as a centre for teaching about the Commonwealth, there would be no reprieve. And I knew next to nothing about education.

In our galleries there were permanent exhibitions on every Commonwealth country and every colony. They were inevitably old-fashioned by the modern standards set by the Festival of Britain, and consisted mainly of mahogany show-cases full of exhibits of economic products and arts and crafts. But there were

M

also many of those beautiful, partly painted, partly modelled scenes, which are known as dioramas. These exhibitions were open to the public and our visitors included thousands of school-children, who were brought in parties by their teachers to learn about the Commonwealth from our guide-lecturers.

There was a fine, if rather shabby, art gallery and a big glass-roofed hall, both intended for temporary exhibitions. Neither of them was very often used. In a small cinema documentary films about the Commonwealth were shown daily, free of charge. We had a big library of books which were mostly out of date, and a stock of filmstrips and slides for lending to schools, but many of these were out of date too. At the bookstall we sold 'readers', pamphlets, wall-charts and other teaching aids about Common-wealth countries, including some which we had produced ourselves.

About 5,000 lectures a year were being given in schools all over the country by a panel of speakers who had all lived in the countries about which they talked. The previous Director, Sir Harry Lindsay, had just begun to arrange one-day study-conferences for sixth forms on various aspects and problems of Commonwealth affairs. Two of these had been organized in 1952.

It did not require more than a glance to see that the foundations on which we must build were already there. Some of them, especially the cinema, the lectures and the conferences, were good. All we would have to do to prove our case was to develop and modernize what we already had and did. For that we only needed an enthusiastic staff, and money. Mercifully we would not have to branch out at this stage into new educational fields, which in England are no place for the amateur.

The staff was enthusiastic but we were clearly not likely to get a bigger grant-in-aid from the Government until we had shown that we could make good use of it, and there was very little time. This was the challenge, and, in essence, it was very like many of the challenges District Officers had had to face in Africa twenty years before, when they so often had to meet urgent needs without professional skills and without any money.

Nineteen fifty-three was Coronation year, when all the

Commonwealth would be in London. So we collected seven small temporary exhibitions on various Commonwealth themes, which the owners let us have for nothing, and put them up in the glass-roofed hall. An exhibition of paintings by Commonwealth artists living in London was put into the art gallery. From flag-staffs on the lawn flew a row of Commonwealth flags; they looked gay and brave, but very small against the smoke-darkened pile of the building massed under its high tower.

The peace of Kensington was destroyed by the massed pipe-bands of the Gurkhas marching and skirling up and down the street. On another day we added to its gaiety by having South African boys and girls in *voortrekker* costumes dancing on the lawn.

In fact very few visitors came near Kensington that summer. They were all so entranced by the decorations in the West End. Still, our attempts at showmanship were at least evidence that the Institute was very much alive.

Meantime the lecture service for schools had begun to grow and more study-conferences were being organized.

We also began to invite artists from other Commonwealth countries to come and exhibit their works in the old art gallery. During the next ten years 120 exhibitions were held, some good and some not so good. If the gallery never achieved a high reputation in London, the Institute was certainly able to give encouragement to painters and sculptors from many under-developed countries, to whom the mere fact of having had an exhibition in London was important.

Almost immediately the Government relented. Not only did they give us a reprieve but altered our constitution so as to give us more freedom of action. The Institute had always been a grant-aided organization with the British Government providing most of the money, but also with small token grants from every Commonwealth and Colonial Government. The Board of Governors included the Commonwealth High Commissioners in London but its President was the British Minister of Education and his Ministry exercised a tight control over both policy and purse-strings. A Committee of Inquiry under Lord Tweedsmuir had recommended, in 1952, that the Institute should have an independent Chairman instead of the overburdened Minister as President. This idea was approved and in 1953 the late Viscount Hudson, who had been Minister of Agriculture in Churchill's Cabinet, accepted the appointment. Lord Hudson, although he had retired from politics, was used to power and with a combination of ruthlessness, bullying and charm he had a useful habit of getting his own way. He had great faith in the future of the Commonwealth and its importance to the world and he believed that the Institute might become one of the chief means of strengthening the ties between its peoples.

'We are going to do this', he said to me. 'We need a new building and enough money and we will get both. I have never yet let lack of money prevent me from doing something worthwhile. Money is only a tool and you can always', he added, with a Churchillian echo, 'get the tools to do a job.' For four years he was my leader, ally and friend.

With an independent Chairman, the Governors, most of whom were High Commissioners, were now more free to decide their own policy and, under Lord Hudson's leadership, the future of the Institute was soon assured. The Government said we could have a new building and offered us a choice of several sites. In 1956 it was decided to build the new Institute by Holland Park and a Bill was promised which would provide both for the new building and for the long overdue change of our name to the 'Commonwealth Institute'. Meantime a small Institute had been opened in Scotland, run by a Scottish committee on a semi-autonomous basis. The British Government's grant-in-aid for the London Institute had, in four years, risen from £13,000 to £40,000. (By 1964 it was £168,000.)

Lord Hudson's death, while on a visit to Rhodesia early in 1957, was a tragic blow. He had saved the Institute from extinction and had successfully carried through all the difficult preliminary negotiations for the new building. He had enjoyed the battles, as any old warrior would, but how much more keenly would he have enjoyed the planning and building of the new Institute as an expression, not of imperialism, but of the new

Commonwealth of today and tomorrow. It was up to us to try to make his dream come true.

Lord Hudson was succeeded as Chairman by the Earl of Dundee. He brought with him the same vision and the same enthusiasm and for four years helped us through the next stage of planning the new building and its exhibitions. When, in 1961, having become a Minister in the Government, he felt he ought to resign, building had already begun.

The planning of every great public building which has ever been put up, and of every exhibition which has ever been made, must always have been an exciting project to those who were immediately concerned in it. For us, I think, it was particularly so because we had such a rare opportunity given to us and an almost unique challenge.

The opportunity was that of planning, in London, a big building on an open site surrounded, not by other buildings with which ours would have to harmonize, but by trees. Architects are rarely given such freedom as this in the centre of a great city. The challenge was to design a great exhibition hall for one precise purpose — the display of permanent exhibitions on all the countries of the Commonwealth in a building which must itself express their forward-looking faith and optimism. Nobody, so far as we knew, had ever had the chance to design anything quite like this in London since, perhaps, the old Institute itself had been designed by Colcutt sixty years before to express the pride and glory of Victorian imperialism.

All good architects begin by saying to their clients 'What do you want this building to do?' Ours, Sir Robert Matthew, Johnson Marshall & Partners, made two suggestions; first, that before they even began to formulate their ideas or to draw any sketches, I should produce for them a paper setting out, in the greatest possible detail, all that we wanted to do in every part of the building, almost down to the position of the last coat-hook; secondly, that we should straight away choose and appoint the designer of the permanent exhibitions so that he could also be in on the planning of the exhibition hall right from the start. We promptly appointed Mr. James Gardner, C.B.E., whose British

Pavilion at the Brussels World Fair was just then being so highly praised. From then on we all worked as a close-knit team. The result is there for others to judge, and any shortcomings there may be in it are nobody's fault but ours. All good architecture must be based on, and its beauty spring from, function, and this law, at least, was faithfully obeyed. The design of the building enables us to carry out its many purposes with great convenience, and almost the only difficulties we experience are due to the fact that we are now using it for many new purposes which we had not even imagined when I wrote that first paper setting out our needs.

The design of the diamond-shaped exhibition block was unique, not only because of its great hyperbolic roof, which was the largest and most intricate of its kind in the country, but also in its interior planning, which was designed as precisely as possible to fit the exhibitions themselves. Usually the unfortunate designer has to fit his exhibitions into an existing building or one which an architect has already planned before he himself was appointed and available for consultation.

Our biggest headache was, of course, finance, as is always the case when the taxpayers' money is being used. The British Government gave us enough money to put up a building, plain and unadorned, but we wanted something more than this. Our new Institute would be the first building in the world to represent the unity in diversity which is the Commonwealth, and express its meaning. For such a purpose it must be beautiful and made of fine materials.

Contributions to the cost of building the old Institute had come from all over the Empire. The new Institute should also be a co-operative effort by the peoples of the Commonwealth. So we appealed to them to contribute gifts in kind. The response was wonderful. Copper came from Northern Rhodesia, aluminium from Canada, rubber for flooring from Malaysia, and fine timbers from all over the Commonwealth.

Almost more complicated than the planning and financing of the building was the task of designing and constructing the exhibitions themselves. There were to be forty-four of these altogether, each showing a different country with its own distinctive character, and yet all designed in a single visual harmony. This was a sufficient challenge for any designer, but it was also complicated by the fact that twenty of the smaller exhibitions had already been recently modernized by ourselves at the old Institute. These had, somehow, to be adapted and incorporated among the other twenty-three new exhibitions which Gardner was to design. In addition, Canada wanted to design and build its own exhibition and ship it over. Visual harmony was going to be a problem.

The team was soon joined by Mr. Harold Midgley, O.B.E., himself a designer of distinction, who came in as research-worker and script-writer. Together, we three worked on the exhibitions for five years, from 1957 to 1962, in close consultation with the Commonwealth High Commissioners, each of whose Governments, with the help of grants from local industries and other sources, paid for its own exhibition.

For my part, I found that almost everything I had ever learned came in useful. I sometimes wonder whether I could have done my share of the job at all if I had not been an amateur jack-of-all-trades. I cannot tell, but I am sure that any man who is given something to do when he is fifty which calls for all his knowledge and experience and gives him a great deal more of both is very fortunate indeed. I know I was, and I was particularly lucky because I was allowed an almost completely free hand. My chairmen, governors and committees could not have been kinder or more helpful. If they had not been so, and if we who had to get the job done had been continually subjected to carping criticism and negative interference, the project would have failed.

Our new Chairman in 1961 was (and still is in 1965) Sir James Robertson. He had until recently been the first Governor-General of Nigeria and had seen that vast country through to independence. He is a great man and was, of course, well used to handling District Officers and swift to encourage their enthusiasms. If the home-bred Civil Servants in Whitehall sometimes thought me an *enfant terrible*, liable to fearful indiscretions, neither Sir James nor the High Commissioners, to most of whom the District Officer

was also a familiar animal, ever seemed to think so. At intervals
they smiled, patted me on my greying head, as it were, solved
money problems for me and backed me whenever I ran into any
trouble. I shall always be grateful to them.

Many of the Institute's staff have been there all their working
lives. Others, all professionals, we recruited as our work expanded, including four or five trained and experienced teachers
who were retiring early from service in the colonies as these
became independent. All of us have, I hope, grown in stature as
the work of the Institute has grown. These men and women
were, by 1960, carrying nearly all the responsibility for the
running of our educational activities on their own shoulders,
which left me free to work on the new Institute. If they had not
done this so well, we should, again, have failed. The only trouble
was that some of them were so enthusiastic and so successful in
developing the services for which they were responsible that
we were always understaffed and they were always overworked.
They ensured the future of the Institute and have kept me sane,
and I have no doubt we will continue to be understaffed and they
overworked until we all retire. That is always the price of
enthusiasm in the public service, and some of us have been paying
it, without thinking about it very much, all our lives.

In the early stages, until the design of the building had been
settled, Gardner, the architects and I were closeted frequently
together and I began to experience, for the first time in my life,
the pleasure of watching first-class professional minds and trained
imaginations busy with creative work. It is easy enough for the
amateur to build dream castles in the air, but when these are
brought down to earth they so easily collapse for lack of technical
know-how. It is quite a different matter when the creative
professional starts to use his imagination. His ideas are disciplined
by much knowledge and much experience. The measure of his
quality is an ability, within these limitations, to create what is
new, evocative and good to look at, as well as practical.

Good professionals respect each other. They bow to each other's
expertise and if they are very good they can, because they have
no false pride, move to and fro across the mutual frontier of their

skills and, without apology, offer each other ideas. There is evidence of this in the design of the exhibition block where Gardner's desire for dramatic visual effects modified many of the architects' ideas, and where the architects' cherished plan for a great hyperbolic roof was agreed to, although it did make Gardner's planning of the exhibitions high up under it on the top gallery much more difficult. During the later stages, when construction had begun and my work with the architects was virtually over, I found myself working more closely and continuously with Gardner, and as time went on we became good friends as well as colleagues.

The experience of working with such men was immensely satisfying and the constant excitement of it made light of those gruelling years. I even came to enjoy editing and sometimes composing the texts and legends for the exhibitions, which is an exercise in compression that would have driven even Tacitus to despair.

At last, however, in September 1962, the end was in sight. In fact it loomed terrifyingly close. We had to move all our possessions out of the old Institute on 3rd September. Men were waiting, with sledge-hammers poised, to knock the building down. The new Institute was finished more or less — and it had taken only just over two years to build — but carpenters and electricians still swarmed all over it; only about half of the new furniture had been delivered; the seven firms of contractors who were building the exhibitions had only completed about seventy per cent of them, and the Queen was due to perform the opening ceremony on 6th November. None of the complicated staffwork needed for a Royal opening to be attended by eight hundred and fifty very distinguished guests had even been started.

The Deputy Director took charge of the whole operation of moving us from the old building, and it was especially during those last few desperate weeks that she and all my other colleagues showed their quality. They have always, before and since, earned for the Institute a high reputation for helpful efficiency and kindness. At that time they all showed remarkable endurance and a cheerful willingness to shoulder practical responsibility, not only in their normal jobs but in new ones which were entirely strange to them. They took off my shoulders the whole responsibility for dismantling the acres of exhibitions in the old building, for disposing of, or moving, thousands of exhibits, piles of library books and mountains of furniture and equipment. They chivvied dealers and contractors, dealt with all the problems of an enormous house-move and protected me from all comers. They also kept the conferences and lectures in the schools all over the country going without a break. I dared not ask them how tired they were. They might have told me. But I knew how much they were doing and how much the upheaval meant to them.

For those who had worked all their lives in the building it was hard to see so many of the old familiar exhibits go, and worse still to see the demolition gangs move in and bring the exhibition galleries crashing down before we had even gone. They had nursed these exhibitions for so many years and some of them had spent many long war-time nights guarding them against incendiary bombs and other perils.

Regrets were sharp, but they were mercifully short. On the day after we moved I found one head of department standing at the window of his office looking out on the lawn and the trees and the sparkling blue glass of the new exhibition block. 'To think', he said, 'that for thirty years I have seen nothing out of my windows except pigeons on a dirty slate roof.'

By so nobly taking over the move, my colleagues set me free for the whole of that last six weeks to concentrate on getting the exhibitions finished and preparing for the opening, to concern myself with the future and not with tearing up the past. So I moved at once into my new office, all among the carpenters and electricians, spattered paint and packing-cases.

I do not remember very much about those hectic days, but I can recall one agonizing moment. I had been downstairs to watch some of our men struggling to move from a lorry into the lift a large bronze statue by Henry Moore. It was to be the centre-piece of the opening exhibition in the art gallery. They had rigged up a block and tackle, but even so they were having a hard struggle, so massive and heavy was the sculpture. I remembered the mover's man who is supposed to have said, 'I like moving 'enery Moore. You can get your 'ook in the 'oles.'

Now, as I was standing on the top gallery in the exhibition block, someone handed me a note. It was from the architects to tell me that the weight of this statue was slightly greater than the load-bearing capacity of the art gallery floor. While I was still absorbing this ominous warning, the whole exhibition block shivered under the impact of a series of deafening crashes and rumblings, like the sound of an earthquake on television. I closed my eyes in horror and saw the Henry Moore plunging through the floor of the art gallery into the stalls of the cinema beneath. When I opened them I saw instead a gang of men far below me emptying rocks out of oil drums on to the floor of Canada. They were to make part of the scenery.

I remember checking endless lists, endless invitation cards — whom had we forgotten? — and endless copy for the captions in the exhibitions. There were crises every day, though what they were about I now have no idea, and in the small hours I would find myself giving food and drink to exhausted artists. They were trying to finish their murals in the quiet of the night when the workmen had all gone home. The rest is blurred by confusion and noise and lack of sleep. Yet everything was miraculously finished by midnight on the day before the opening and the great occasion went off without a visible hitch.

In her speech the Queen said: 'It is just seventy-five years since my great-great-grandmother, Queen Victoria, laid the foundation stone of the old Imperial Institute. Since that great occasion, the development of the Institute into its present form as the Commonwealth Institute has mirrored the development of the Commonwealth itself. Seventy-five years ago it was the Queen-Empress and the Imperial Institute; today it is the Head of the Commonwealth opening the new building of the Commonwealth Institute. We in the Commonwealth form an association of peoples as well as of governments; and our association cannot prosper to the full, unless ordinary people in each country really care about what is happening in the others. It is the thread of personal concern and understanding between individual people that weaves the strong fabric of the modern Commonwealth.

'It is in the name of all the peoples of the Commonwealth that I declare this building open.'

Then Her Majesty let fall the new white silk flag of the Institute which was draped over the commemorative plaque. Our dream had all come true. We opened to the public at ten o'clock the next morning and started our new life.

CHAPTER 15

New Horizons

WHEN I came to the Institute in 1953 the modern Common-wealth had, with the independence of India and Pakistan in 1947 and of Ceylon in 1948, begun to emerge. Already the coloured population of the independent member countries outnumbered the white by ten to one. Already there were republics which acknowledged the Queen not as Sovereign but as the 'symbol of their free association and, as such, Head of the Commonwealth'. The independence of India and Pakistan and the acceptance of India as a republic within the Commonwealth had been the turning point in its history. It was now recognized that the grant of independence to all the major dependencies could not always wait upon their attainment of economic viability. Educational standards could not always be high enough to give them Civil Services comparable with the Colonial Service, nor, perhaps, political stability. The wind of change was stirring and had begun to blow old ideas away, but a few years were yet to pass before it rose to gale force. In 1953 Malaya was still busy suppressing Communism and trying to forge some sort of unity between its Malayan and Chinese inhabitants. It was not to be in-dependent until 1957, the same year in which Kwame Nkrumah was to become Prime Minister of an independent Ghana and blow the spark of nationalism into flame all over Africa.

At the old Institute, therefore, we had four relatively quiet years in which to accustom ourselves to the new conception of the Commonwealth, and to the realization that colonialism was dying and would doubtless be replaced by something different. For those of us who had been in the Colonial Service this adjustment was not so very difficult to make because we had, since the war, been busy trying to help colonial peoples towards independence. The process was merely being speeded up.

It has taken longer to make the mental adjustment needed to realize that the governments and peoples of the newly independent countries are not ex-colonials still principally concerned with their relations with Britain, but are nations in their own right, determined to strike out on their own into a complicated modern world. This has involved a reversal of long-cherished attitudes and the always very difficult process of trying to see the world and ourselves through other peoples' eyes.

If we could not achieve this we could not do our job, which is to help the people, and especially the young people, of Britain to see the Commonwealth not as it used to be, but as it is. All of us are concerned to help teachers in particular to understand the new conception of the Commonwealth as a voluntary association of completely independent peoples, to whom Britain is not so important as their neighbours. The Commonwealth is no longer a wheel with Britain as its hub, but rather, as Prince Philip has said, a kind of lattice. It is its own league of nations, more effective than the greater League because it is an association of peoples and not merely of governments and because it has grown out of history and is not an artificial creation.

To understand this, to realize the potential of the Commonwealth and to help its peoples to join in building their future on this foundation, is one of the many challenges which face our country. The Institute exists to help our people to meet it. I wonder if we can?

It is true that we no longer, even among ourselves, have any inclination to talk about the 'British Commonwealth', which it is not, and that we can sometimes even think of Britain as objectively as we can of Canada or Sierra Leone, but for most of us this objectivity is still a conscious process. The adjustment is not yet complete.

For me it has been greatly eased by the frequent journeys I have made since 1955 to almost every country in the Commonwealth. Especially, perhaps, because I visit these countries as a representative not of the British Government, but of what is, in effect, a pan-Commonwealth organization. Everywhere my colleagues and I have been welcomed by Commonwealth

Governments, and almost everywhere we have been their guests. I have had many opportunites to learn to see the problems of the Commonwealth through the eyes of the people concerned and also, perhaps, to see the Commonwealth itself as they see it.

It is not very difficult to understand how all governments and most educated people throughout the Commonwealth see it. They believe in it because it helps them, because they feel that they can and should contribute to it, and because it has no political implications.

It is, I suppose, much easier for us to take a detached view of the problems of the Commonwealth than it is for its politicians and Civil Servants, because they are all immersed in their own countries' problems and policies and must form judgments and make decisions. We must try to understand their problems but we do not have to, and indeed must not, pass judgment. We watch from the touchline and may not take sides. There are, after all, two sides to the Kashmir problem between India and Pakistan, to the unhappy relations between the Sinhalese and Tamils in Ceylon, and to the racial and political problem in Rhodesia.

Only recently in Ghana I was pressed very hard to state the 'view of the Institute' on Rhodesia. I explained that we had no views, but were only concerned with presenting at our study-conferences both sides of the case as objectively as possible and leaving the students to make up their own minds. My passionately committed inquisitor found this very difficult to understand. But the Commonwealth Governments whom we serve understand it perfectly and would not have it otherwise. Our chief difficulty in studying these matters and in teaching about them is to take off our grandmotherly British spectacles while we do so. This does not, of course, mean that our loyalty to Britain has become diffused and weakened. It has merely become extended to the Commonwealth as a whole as our horizons have widened.

I realized most clearly, I think, how deeply we had become concerned with the interests of the Commonwealth as a whole when South Africa left the Commonwealth. Her departure was no surprise. Indeed, it seemed so inevitable that James Gardner had not begun to draw any plans for a South African exhibition in the new Institute and we had already discussed how to extend the Nigerian and Rhodesian sections to fill the vacant space which would be left between them. For sentimental and historical reasons the withdrawal of South Africa would be a tragedy, but we had already faced it.

For those of us who had such happy memories of the country and its peoples, going back thirty years or more, and who remembered Smuts as one of the truest friends our country ever had and as one of the prophets of the Commonwealth, this was going to be a bitter pill to swallow. Yet it had to be done, because we knew that a principle was at stake on which neither Verwoerd's Government on the one hand, nor the rest of the Commonwealth on the other, could be expected to compromise.

I was in Wellington when the news came and I asked my New Zealand friends what they felt about it. Did they agree with those who said that this would lead to the break-up of the Commonwealth because the principle of non-interference by its Governments in each other's internal affairs seemed to have been abandoned? 'On the contrary', they said, 'there is no other issue so important as *apartheid*. Everybody will be more careful than ever now to mind their own business, and to tolerate no racialism. It is a challenge to all of us to act on that principle.' This is how I had come to feel. The Commonwealth has not been weakened. The challenge remains.

Loyalty to the Commonwealth itself has, in my case, been a natural growth, because the reality of the Commonwealth as an association of *peoples*, of millions of men, women and children, who believe in it, has been impressed upon me more and more clearly in every country I have visited. The process began in 1955 when I went on a short tentative journey to Malta. Since then I have been to Cyprus, India, Pakistan, Ceylon, Malaysia (including Singapore, Sabah and Sarawak), Brunei, Australia, New Zealand, Fiji, Canada, Rhodesia, Zambia, Malawi, Tanzania, Kenya, Uganda, Sierra Leone and Ghana.

These journeys still go on. None of them is undertaken merely to learn more about the countries and their peoples, though this in every case has been a major purpose. There is always business to see to. It includes seeking grants for new exhibitions and exhibits to put in them, arranging for art exhibitions to be sent to London, and talking to Ministers and heads of universities. It also includes looking for information material, maps, wall-charts and school textbooks which could be used in British schools, encouraging Ministries of Education to promote the study of the Commonwealth in their own schools, lecturing and broadcasting and talking to as many teachers and as many other ordinary men and women as possible. They are always busy journeys and, of course, far too hurried. In 1961 I went, in actual fact, 'Round the World in Eighty Days' (including two Good Fridays, one hot one in Fiji and one snowy one in Vancouver, all in twenty-four hours). Except between planes, I did not set foot outside the Commonwealth.

The drawback of jet-travel is, of course, that one is seldom able to see a country as a whole. Each is remembered rather as a series of local pictures, unconnected with each other. Bombay one has seen, and Madras. What lies in between? I always try to spend at least part of each visit travelling by road, but even so, the Commonwealth is for me, as for any traveller, far too kaleidoscopic a series of impressions.

We used to have an old saying in Africa that only two kinds of people should be allowed to write books about it, — those who had spent a life-time there, and those who had seen it in a week. I have not yet tried to write a travel book, but I can see that there is some truth in this saying. The instant impression created on a detached, eager and reasonably well-informed visitor is often true, sometimes surprisingly so to the local residents, who have long ago lost sight of the wood for the trees.

All this travel has helped enormously in our work at the Institute and has been of value over and over again in our study-conferences and in all our teaching about the Commonwealth. For me, this expresses itself most easily in vivid memories of personal contacts with people.

I remember, for instance, a very young student of Agra University. We were sitting together looking at the opalescent shimmer of the Taj Mahal in the warm moonlight when he

N

fractured the breathless silence of that supreme, if hackneyed, experience by asking:

'Who are you? Are you married? How many sons have you? What is your job?' Very Indian.

I told him. He said: 'The Commonwealth? I've never heard of it. It sounds like some organization for sharing riches.' Out of the mouths of babes!

I remember being taken out into the palm-fringed paddy fields inland from Madras to see the Village Aid programme in action. This is the Indian version of the Community Development I had helped to start at Fort Jameson in 1938. Here was a team of young men and women trying to bring the twentieth century to a group of villages as primitive as any I had known in Africa and much more hungry. When I told them that I had once done the very same work, they cried, 'Oh! So you're one of us. We were going to show you our best village, but now we will show you the worst. Perhaps you can help.' So we went off happily together and I spent a nostalgic morning sitting on the verandah of a hut talking to a circle of squatting villagers and admiring, believe it or not, that newly invented miracle, the family pit latrine. We were of the same trade, those young Indians and I. And it is all part of the Commonwealth that we so comfortably shared the same language, the same thoughts and purpose, and the same kind of experience, professional or amateur.

Then there was the young Political Officer with whom I talked at the northern end of the Khyber Pass.

'How', I asked him, as we stood there looking at the Afghan sentry beyond the frontier, 'do you deal with the Pathans?'

'Well', he said — I remember his actual words and his faultless English — 'We do not fight them, as you did, because we are all Muslims. That would be a sin.' Then he added, 'But they still enjoy their blood-feuds. I tell them that they can "create" as much as they like, so long as they don't "create" near my road.'

'Create'? For a second I thought it must be the ghost of an Englishman who spoke.

'Is there much traffic on the road from Khabul?' I asked.

'You'd be surprised! Especially the tourists. We even get them on scooters all the way from Europe. Only yesterday', he added, 'I had a young Irishman. He had an Eire passport and I had to refuse to let him in because he had no visa for Pakistan. "But you must let me in", he said. "We are in the Commonwealth, more or less." I told him just what I thought of people who tried to take all the advantages of the Commonwealth without accepting its responsibilities. I locked him up in that hut down there while I got a ruling from Peshawar. Oh yes, they let him in, but he had had a very uncomfortable night.'

That young Political Officer must have been a schoolboy in 1947 and he had probably never been out of Pakistan. I thought of where we were standing as we talked, and of all the history which had been made here in the Khyber Pass, and of this young man and the legacy he had inherited, and of the Commonwealth. As I went down again through those hills, still carved with crests of British regiments, I felt very humble.

I flew over India to East Pakistan and travelled across the delta of the Brahmaputra in a steamer called the *Comet* and there I saw the greatest jute mill in the world, built by the Agha Khan. The manager was a Scotsman from Dundee, but his assistant was a Pakistani who had come from Tanganyika with a very beautiful Pakistani wife, whose home had been in Uganda. (Most of the Muslim Asians in East Africa I remembered are followers of the Agha Khan.) His wife had had four years in London being trained by Constance Spry, and she was a delightful hostess. It is threads crossed like this, I thought, which are the warp and woof of the Commonwealth.

Then there was that village in Ceylon. I was touring the island with a charming and highly cultivated Sinhalese. He had shown me all the rock paintings at Sighariya, which had looked to me like caricatures of court ladies whom the artists had known, and many other crumbling glories of the ancient kings.

Presently we came to a neat and prosperous village full of young farmers and their lovely, silk-clad wives.

'Do you realize', said my guide, 'that all these young people have had a secondary education? They are good farmers and they are not poor.'

'No indeed, this looks like the kind of rural paradise which is the dream of UNESCO.'

'Yes', he said bitterly, 'and it is also the worst hotbed of Communism in Ceylon. These people don't want to go on the land. They want to work in offices and there aren't enough jobs.'

I thought of the State of Kerala in South India where so many graduates were being produced that many of them were glad to be employed as bus-drivers. Kerala had just turned Communist. So? So either you don't educate the peasants and they fall easy prey to Communist propaganda, or you educate too many people too highly and get the same result.

'What are you going to do about it?' I asked.

'Vocational guidance. Direct them into suitable careers.'

Direct them? I sighed again for democracy and was more than ever convinced that the most critical frontier of the free world lay between south-east Asia and China. Nothing that might happen in Africa during the next twenty years would really affect the world as a whole. But here in Asia the issue of freedom is being fought out on such a gigantic scale that the result must tilt the world.

I remember, too, most vividly, the contrast between the Nairobi of 1961, when Jomo Kenyatta was still reviled by many and still exiled in the desert north and everyone was apprehensive because there was no unity in the country and no leadership, and Nairobi in 1964, when Kenyatta had become Prime Minister of an independent Kenya and was astonishing everyone by his statesmanship and sheer capacity.

'I would never have thought it possible', said an elderly retired British general who was my guest at lunch, 'that I should find myself at a farmers' meeting yesterday, cheering for Kenyatta — but I did.'

And I thought of that very different African leader, Julius Nyerere, who had once come to see us at the Institute. He has always been loved by everyone.

I remember seeing two young English girls, in shorts and beautifully tanned, walking down a road in Jesselton, the capital of Sabah in eastern Borneo.

'Who are they?' I asked and I was told that they were two girls from an English grammar school who had come out under the scheme for Voluntary Service Overseas and were living with the Muruts in a longhouse somewhere up in the mountains, teaching the women how to look after their babies.

I saw for myself the tremendous challenge of Australia and the wonderful people who have been bred to meet it, many of them so like Rhodesians in their slow charm and forthrightness, their courage and enthusiasm. I also found that, in spite of the so-called 'White Australia policy' there is no people in the world so little cursed with race prejudice. There are usually about 16,000 astonished Asian students in Australia. They are always astonished because they come expecting to meet this prejudice and all its unpleasant consequences, and they do not find any signs of it at all. They soon feel at home, as any Commonwealth citizen can feel at home in any Commonwealth country. I heard a story on this subject, which I hope is true.

In Sydney, a tough city full of very outspoken people, there is a plate on the dashboard of every taxi which reads — 'Your driver is (say) Mr. W. Smith', and underneath is written, 'Bill'. The good democratic custom is that the passenger sits in front with the driver and, presumably, calls him Bill. Indeed it would be foolish to sit in the back because Sydney taxi-drivers are very exhilarating company.

One day a certain official from Pakistan arrived in Sydney and picked up a taxi at the docks. Feeling rather nervous in this strange and frightening 'White Australia' he crept into the back seat and told the driver his destination. Bill turned round and grinned at him.

'And just who the hell d'you think you are, mate? You come and sit in front with me.'

Because I never felt strange anywhere, all these memories serve to bring home to me the true meaning of the Commonwealth far more clearly than all the articles, political pronouncements and books on the subject that I have ever read. Perhaps in our teaching at the Institute we can never hope really to explain the elusive reality and strength of the 'silken bond' (to use Nehru's famous phrase) of human relationships which binds the Commonwealth together. At least we make sure that whoever speaks about the Commonwealth on our behalf knows at least one part of it personally — knows what its people are like, how they live and something of how they think, and knows, too, its heat or cold, the smell of its rain and dust, all its beauty and its squalor.

My travels have, as all travel should be, also been immensely enriching. A Hellenic cruise is one unforgettable experience, and a tour of India which includes the Taj Mahal and the Red Fort at Delhi is another, but who can say which stores the mind and the memory more fully? I have been lucky enough to do both, and in my store are not only Delphi and the rose-red city of Jhaipur, but so many other vivid memories gathered from the corners of the world. Nor are my travels finished yet. I do not want to smell again, though no doubt I shall, the reeking slums of Bombay, nor to feel again the searing heat of a desert wind in an Australian summer, but I do want to go fishing in the New Zealand Alps. I saw them only from an aeroplane, lying like a white and golden frieze high above the pale blue silk of the Tasman Sea. That was not enough. I hope, too, if I am very lucky, to wake again at dawn in Sabah and see Mount Kinabalu rising copper-coloured from purple shadow into a clear green sky. But then shall I ever have my fill of mountains, or the sea?

CHAPTER 16

In My End is My Beginning

WHEN I came to the end of the last chapter of *The Story of Northern Rhodesia*[1] in 1941, I realized that what I had been writing was in fact not the last but only the first chapter of a story which had hardly started, so instead of writing THE END beneath it, I wrote THE BEGINNING. Now I find myself in much the same position, though in this book I have not been trying to write the story of the development of the British Empire into the modern Commonwealth, but merely to record my own experience within the setting of that story.

When I was young the Empire, for whose service we were moulded, offered us an attractive and useful life, opportunities for adventure and, at the end, a pension. Today, for young people in all Commonwealth countries, the underdeveloped world and the Commonwealth in particular offer a rather less attractive life, or so it seems to us who were sheltered by the *Pax Britannica*, but opportunities for service and adventure even greater than those we had nearly half a century ago. The story of the Commonwealth has only just begun.

My own story, too, although the new Institute is a dream come true, has not yet ended. After the Queen had opened our new building, many of my friends said to me, 'Now you can sit back and enjoy it all.' The hard fact is that, largely as a result of having a fine new building, the work has continued to expand so fast that none of us has ever worked harder. Half a million visitors come to us each year. We have had as many as a thousand schoolchildren arriving in coaches in a single morning, all expecting to be taught about the Commonwealth. More than eight thousand talks are being given in the schools each year, and the annual total of study-conferences in teacher-training and other

[1] See p. 117.

colleges of further education and for sixth forms and secondary modern schools has risen to about a hundred. We are having to learn how to select exhibitions for our art gallery which represent only what is best in contemporary art from all over the Commonwealth; how to attract good singers, dancers and musicians to our theatre; how to organize receptions for Commonwealth Governments in our exhibition galleries; how to publish a Commonwealth Institute journal which will be useful to teachers who are interested in the Commonwealth; how to run a modern reference library. There seems to be no end to the variety of new ventures we are asked to undertake nor to the new skills we have to learn. Perhaps the story of the Institute is also only just beginning. That will depend on whether the far greater dream of the Commonwealth itself comes true.

There seems to have been, in Britain, during the early sixties a cleavage of opinion on this subject. It began to show itself very markedly when the Government was trying to take us into the European Common Market. So far as the economic possibilities were concerned there did not seem, at first, to be any conflict between the interests of Britain and the other Commonwealth nations, if only because a more prosperous Britain could give more help to the underdeveloped countries. When, however, it became apparent that one of the objectives of the Western Europeans was political unity, doubts began to grow. It was soon clear that many people were not prepared to jeopardize Britain's special relationship with the rest of the Commonwealth by entering into any kind of political union with Western Europe. On the day that the Common Market talks finally broke down, because de Gaulle had slammed the door in our faces, Lord Beaverbrook's headline, 'Glory, Glory Hallelujah!' echoed the feelings of thousands who did not know very much about the political or economic affairs of the Commonwealth, but did believe in it with their hearts.

Meanwhile, this controversy, coupled with current disputes between some Commonwealth countries, unexpected and 'un-British' political developments in some of them, and the disproportionate power being built up by the African countries in the United Nations, combined to produce a mood of cynicism and depression among politicians, and, I fear, most of the clever commentators on radio and television and some columnists. They seemed to be trying to write the Commonwealth off.

Yet the more I travelled through the Commonwealth the more convinced I became that this pessimism was not reflected among educated people anywhere else, except perhaps among a few Canadians and some of the distracted Europeans in Rhodesia. On the contrary I felt increasingly that they believed in the Commonwealth, and were much distressed by what they understandably took to be the prevailing opinion in Britain.

It is, of course, not surprising that some people in Britain should be dismayed by the erosion of parliamentary democracy and other more sinister happenings, which they had hardly expected, in some of the new countries. Inevitably they were still seeing them through British eyes. It is, after all, a traumatic experience for any people to lose nearly all their imperial power in little more than ten years. Happily the British have always been pragmatic and adaptable. If we were not, neither the steady, experimental development of our colonial policy, nor the creation of the Commonwealth out of the Empire could ever have happened. That it is not a 'British Commonwealth' but a Commonwealth of free and equal nations is already being accepted.

Many do, however, find it hard to believe that a Commonwealth which is not based on British power can hold together. Others believe that it can, but all too few in either camp really seem to understand what the new type of Commonwealth association is and what it is not.

Neither emotional pessimism nor wishful thinking will get us anywhere. We must start by knowing the facts. In 1964, therefore, I ventured to write a short, highly condensed and almost entirely factual pamphlet called *What is the Commonwealth?* We planned to distribute it from the Institute, free and as widely as possible, hoping to help at least some people to a clearer understanding of the myths and the realities of the Commonwealth. Within a year nearly half a million copies had been issued, both in Britain and overseas. This pamphlet still seems to be valid and, since it really sums up, to this point in time, the Commonwealth story which forms the background to this book, I have included the most recent edition of it as an Appendix.

The problems which bedevil the Commonwealth at any given moment must also be understood and faced. Some of them rate the news bulletins and some of them, such as the social effects of large-scale immigration, are on our own doorstep. Others are not so familiar to us in this country but they nevertheless give statesmen sleepless hours. It is, for instance, only too clear that the internal political pressures on the Prime Ministers of many newly independent countries, especially in Africa, are always strong enough to threaten revolution. The combination of these and even tougher economic difficulties may prove too much for them. The communal problem, whether between Sinhalese and Tamils, Muslims and Hindus, white and black Africans, or French and other Canadians, is nearly everywhere unresolved and dangerous. Most serious of all is the growing gap between the haves and the have-nots. As in the old song, 'There's nothing surer, the rich get richer and the poor have children.'

Yet I have learned that people, no matter how poor, no matter what the colour of their skins, are more often kind than cruel, more inclined to be decent than dishonest. If they are left alone to make up their own minds they can be both moderate and sensible. The curse which lies upon our world is the exploitation of men's ignorance and the poisoning of their minds, often in the sacred cause of 'truth' and 'realism', which are so often only one side of truth, and that exaggerated. Bad news is always news and good news is nothing to shout about. Nehru, in the speech in which he suggested that 1965 should be an International Co-operation Year, put it like this: 'We live in a world of conflicts and yet the world goes on undoubtedly because of the co-operation of nations and individuals . . . even today between countries which are opposed to each other in the political fields, there is a vast amount of co-operation. Little is known or little is said about this co-operation that is going on, but a great deal is said about every point of conflict, and so the world is full of this idea that the conflicts go on and we live on the verge of disaster. Perhaps it would be a truer picture if the co-operating elements in the world today were put forward and we were made to think that the world depends on co-operation and not on conflict.' Those who have some faith in the ability of men's virtue and intelligence to survive a Hitler and a Stalin in our century, are not necessarily to be derided for their optimism.

What emerges, perhaps, from that little pamphlet is my belief that the essence of the Commonwealth does not lie in political or trade relationships, but in the unchanging quality of people, in the millions of personal links which are the result of a shared heritage of ideas and institutions, and shared experience.

The Commonwealth is essentially a partnership between old friends who understand each other and are used to each other's ways. It is becoming more and more regionalized as its peoples in various parts of the world gather their friends about them to face their common problems and it is none the worse for that. The Colombo Plan is, as an idea and a model for the future, more significant than the economic aid which Britain gives to this particular country or that, however much greater the total of that aid may be.

When India was attacked by China, and Britain immediately offered her arms, I had telephone calls from Indians to say how grateful they were and how glad they were to have such old and trustworthy friends. Similar help was asked for and promptly given when the troops in East Africa mutinied, when Malaysia was 'confronted' by Indonesia, and when trouble broke out again between Greeks and Turks in Cyprus, though that proved to be as thankless a task for us as anything else we had ever tried to do in that ill-starred island. But it was, perhaps, a portent of the future that when Julius Nyerere had disbanded his mutinous army and the British troops had withdrawn from Tanganyika, they were replaced by Nigerians; and that Tunku Abdul Rahman, Prime Minister of Malaysia, sought additional help against Sukarno from Australia and New Zealand, and was given it.

The Prime Ministers' Conference of 1964 may well have marked another turning-point in the story of the Commonwealth. If its recommendations are quickly and sincerely acted upon, it will. It certainly confounded the prophets of gloom. The Africans were sensibly moderate in their political and economic demands; India and Pakistan had private talks about Kashmir, and President Ayub Khan went out of his way to make conciliatory pleas for co-operation; Abdul Rahman was able to enlist support and sympathy for his stand against Sukarno. The old magic was still at work, still effective, and during those brilliant summer days, with the Queen's dinner for the Prime Ministers, her garden party, the splendid receptions, and all the colour and gaiety of a great Commonwealth occasion, the silken bond of the Commonwealth was once more seen to be strongly woven.

More important still, perhaps, than the political responsibility shown by the Prime Ministers, was the initiative taken by the new countries. Eight practical suggestions were made to strengthen co-operation between Commonwealth countries. They proposed a Commonwealth Secretariat, the joint training of administrators, more aid for higher education, a Commonwealth Medical Conference, a Commonwealth foundation to foster close co-operation in this and other professional fields and in sport; a Commonwealth satellite communications system; co-operation by several countries in particular economic projects and in general towards the opening of western markets to Commonwealth products; and the holding of the Prime Ministers' Conferences in different capitals.

None of these suggestions is very ambitious and they may not all prove to be practicable, especially the last. For a number of reasons which have nothing to do with politics, the Prime Ministers like coming to London, particularly in June. Nevertheless, all the ideas are important because they show quite clearly that the Prime Ministers recognize the Commonwealth for what it is, a practical working partnership, and that it can, by co-operating in a very wide range of activities, be of increasing value and importance to their peoples and to the world.

I hope that the next Conference, to be held in June 1965, will be equally successful, for already experience has begun to show how useful such practical co-operation can be. Some examples are mentioned in *What is the Commonwealth?* but there are many others.

Among the most fruitful is the co-operation in educational matters. The first Commonwealth Education Conference, held in Oxford in 1958, which launched the postgraduate scholarship scheme, has led to a network of other successful schemes ranging from the supply of teachers to developing countries, to the mass production of cheap textbooks. The Institute is itself a good working example of practical co-operation in this field between Commonwealth Governments, and we are proud to have been in the van of a movement which may affect the future of the Commonwealth association.

If there is a possibility that the 1964 Conference may have marked a real step forward in the Commonwealth affairs, it will not, I think, have been entirely owing to the political experience and skill of the Prime Ministers and the good sense they showed. These qualities could not in themselves have been enough to overcome the dangers which threatened. It seems to me that they succeeded because they wanted to succeed, and because they believed in their hearts that the Commonwealth must be preserved and strengthened. If it were an entirely rational organization which could be easily explained, it could so easily be explained away and lost. But it is not; it is just as much an act of faith which draws its power, as any creed does, from the hearts of men as well as from their thinking. No ideal can endure and no dream come true unless people believe in it with their hearts. It is worth remembering that of the 700,000,000 people in the Commonwealth the vast majority represented by their Prime Ministers at the Conferences are Asians and Africans who do, in general, think most surely and steadfastly with their hearts. The Commonwealth will endure only so long as its peoples believe in it.

This philosophy of practical idealism guides the policy of the leaders of the Commonwealth and also our work at the Institute. I believe that it will, in the long run, be proved to be right. So, at this propitious moment, when our own small dream of a Commonwealth Institute has come true, and the far greater dream of the Commonwealth of the future is beginning to unfold, the time has come when I must write 'The Beginning' rather than 'The End'.

I would not have lived any other life. Some of it has been

exciting, most of it rewarding, and I hope that I have helped to contribute something worth while, here and there.

When I look back now, I am pleased to find that the pictures which rise most clearly from all my memories are not those of the British Empire but of the Commonwealth, which was spun from it on a golden thread of friendship and now lies like a shining scarf across the world. The most vivid memory of them all, perhaps, is that of the summer morning in 1963 when the Head of the Commonwealth brought the President of India to the Institute and, with the High Commissioner for Canada as their host, invited the President to open a national exhibition of contemporary Canadian painting. Such a thing had never happened before and nothing, I believe, could more clearly express the meaning both of the Commonwealth and of the Institute.

London, March 1965

What is the Commonwealth?

*A pamphlet published by the Commonwealth Institute
in 1964 and revised in September 1965*

'The Commonwealth today has reached a point of development which needs to be explained. Nothing quite like it has ever happened before.' H.R.H. THE DUKE OF EDINBURGH

The Commonwealth is a voluntary association of independent nations which were formerly in the British Empire or had been Protectorates or Protected States in treaty relations with the Crown. It also includes those territories and islands, some of them very small, which have not yet attained independence. The independent Commonwealth, however, is not a mere extension of the Empire. It is an experiment in civilised living by many different peoples who share a common heritage of ideals and institutions and whose eyes are fixed not on the past but on the future. They belong to many races and religions and speak a multitude of tongues; they comprise more than a quarter of the world's population and they occupy a quarter of its land surface.

The relationship of each Commonwealth country with the British Empire, and consequently with the Commonwealth which has grown out of it, formed only a part of its own history. For some, like India, it was only a relatively short part; for others, like Australia, it has been almost the whole of it. The story of the Commonwealth ought not to be told solely in terms of the evolution of British imperialism, but as the coming together of peoples into a new relationship through a common experience which they all shared during one period of their histories.

The Commonwealth is important to the world because it provides a working model for effective international and inter-racial co-operation, and because it forms a natural bridge of mutual understanding between the developed and under-developed nations.

INDEPENDENT MEMBERS

Of the independent Member-States of the Commonwealth, some are monarchies and some republics (see below), and there are also dependent territories which may be Crown Colonies (some with full internal self-government), Protectorates, Protected States, or Trust Territories administered on behalf of the United Nations.

The Commonwealth is so continuously experimental and independence is proceeding at such speed that any constitutional classification of its members becomes almost immediately out of date. The following lists show the full Members as at September 1965, with the dates on which they achieved independence:

Countries of which Her Majesty is Queen

Commonwealth of Australia (1901), Britain, Canada (responsible government 1867), Ceylon (1948), Gambia (1965), Jamaica (1962), Malawi (1964), Malta (1964), New Zealand (1907), Sierra Leone (1961), Trinidad and Tobago (1962).

Republics

Cyprus (1960), Ghana (1957), India (1947), Kenya (1963), Nigeria (1960), Pakistan (1947), United Republic of Tanzania (Tanganyika (1961) and Zanzibar (1963)), Zambia (1964). Uganda (1962) has a republican-type constitution, with the Kabaka (King) of the Baganda as President, but prefers to be described as a Sovereign State.

Malaysia

The Federation of Malaya which, in September 1963, was expanded into Malaysia, has its own monarchical Head of State, but, like all other Member countries, recognises The Sovereign as Head of the Commonwealth.

All these countries are independent, equal partners; all, on becoming independent, chose of their own free will to seek full membership of the Commonwealth, and all are free to leave it at any time. Britain has no special constitutional position and no special powers. Britain, Canada,

Malaysia, Sierra Leone and all the other members have exactly the same status. Britain does, however, undoubtedly hold a special position due to the part she played in the creation of the Commonwealth and the consequent existence of long-established facilities in London for consultation and co-operation in social, cultural, financial and economic matters. In no sphere, however, does Britain exercise control.

Many kinds of democratic constitutions are to be found among the independent countries because, being independent, they have been free to choose whatever constitutions they consider best suited to their needs. There are federations, as in Canada, Australia, Nigeria and Malaysia; there are unitary states, as in Britain, New Zealand and Sierra Leone; and in India there is a union of states. Similarly, there is now a wide variety of parliamentary systems, ranging from those in Australia, India, Malaysia, and other countries which closely resemble that of the 'Mother of Parliaments' at Westminster, to the 'one-party' systems being evolved in Ghana, Kenya and Tanzania.

DEPENDENT MEMBERS

There were, in September 1965, twenty-four territories and island groups still dependent on Britain, of which the largest or most populous are Rhodesia, Hong Kong, British Guiana, Mauritius and Fiji. Australia administers Papua and several small islands, as well as the United Nations Trust Territories of New Guinea and Nauru. India has one Protectorate, Sikkim, and also administers some island groups, while New Zealand controls islands in the South Pacific. Britain, Australia, and New Zealand also all have territories on the Antarctic continent.

The Governors of all the British Dependencies are appointed by the Queen and are responsible to the Secretary of State for the Colonies who, in turn, is responsible to the British Parliament, where the ultimate control lies.

Britain's long-established policy of preparing her dependencies for self-government means that their peoples are given more and more control over their own affairs until they have full internal

o

self-government, which is the last state before complete independence. Even in New Guinea and the Solomon Islands the elements of representative government have been introduced by Australia and Britain respectively. Rhodesia has had full internal self-government since 1924. In all cases the political system is largely modelled on that of Britain.

Nearly all the larger dependent territories are likely to achieve their independence before long, though the future of some of the very small ones, such as the Pacific Islands and the Falklands, is more difficult to foresee. Some may federate with larger neighbouring Commonwealth countries, as Sabah, Sarawak and Singapore did with Malaya in 1963; others, such as Fiji, may evolve new forms of association under the British Crown, and yet others may prefer to remain under British protection with full internal self-government.

CONSULTATION AND CO-OPERATION

The Commonwealth is not a political union or federation; it is not a military alliance, and it is not an economic bloc. Nor is it an artificially created association with a constitution, a set of rules and a defined purpose. It is, and this is where its strength lies, a voluntary association, not only of governments but also of peoples, which is rooted in history and has grown up naturally, like a tree. Its peoples are old friends and working partners who understand each other, who have a great deal in common, and who believe that they have much to gain from staying together and something to offer to the rest of the world. They do not need to make rules to govern their dealings with each other, and, indeed, they do not want to do so because they all know that the success of the Commonwealth is largely due to the fact that in carrying out this great experiment its peoples are completely free to adapt it to their constantly changing needs and circumstances.

THE SYMBOL OF UNITY

The only formal link which binds the Commonwealth together is the Queen. Some countries (see above) prefer, after independence to retain her as their own queen. In them she exercises sovereignty not as Queen of Britain, but as Queen of Canada, or Australia, or Sierra Leone, as the case may be. She is represented in those countries by a Governor-General, often a local citizen, who must act on the advice of the local Ministers. Other governments, however, whose peoples are not of British stock, prefer to have one of their own leaders as a Head of State in his own right. They either become republics, with Presidents, or, as in Malaysia, choose one of their own traditional rulers as their King. The Queen does not exercise any sovereignty in these countries, but they all agree to recognise her as 'the symbol of their free association and, as such, the Head of the Commonwealth'. When a country becomes a republic or sets up its own monarchy it makes no practical difference either to its relationship with Britain and the rest of the Commonwealth or to the respect and affection which its people feel for the Queen.

THE SILKEN BOND

The Commonwealth is essentially a working partnership of old friends who value the practical benefits which such a partnership can bring them. On achieving independence all new Commonwealth countries shared in a common heritage of public institutions acquired from Britain and designed to carry the principles of western democracy into practice: parliamentary government, the Rule of Law, an independent judiciary and a civil service divorced from politics. One or two countries, in trying to evolve forms of government which they consider more suited to their needs, have not preserved these institutions intact, but the great majority of Commonwealth governments have done so.

In addition, every Commonwealth country has inherited English as the common language of all educated people, of commerce and of diplomacy. Most important of all perhaps, their education systems are all with certain local exceptions, based on British principles and practice, including the academic freedom of the Universities. The result of all this is that educated people in the Commonwealth share a common intellectual heritage. A Nigerian Prime Minister can not only understand what an Indian Prime Minister is saying, but why he says it. Commonwealth governments do not always agree with each other, but mutual understanding and tolerance are often more important than agreement.

Similarly, the peoples of the Commonwealth have long been accustomed to doing business with each other and have built up vast connections and have adopted the same industrial and commercial practices. There are, throughout the Commonwealth, millions of personal links and friendships between public men and public bodies, between firms and universities and schools and between individuals. Commonwealth citizens can feel 'at home' in other Commonwealth countries. Membership of the Commonwealth has been described by one of its statesmen as 'independence with something added', the 'something added' being the sum of the common ideals and institutions and personal ties which link its peoples together. It was Mr. Nehru who called the sum of them 'the silken bond around the Commonwealth'.

THE PRACTICAL LINKS

The cohesion between the Commonwealth governments is based on constant consultation and exchange of information. They exchange ambassadors, though these are called High Commissioners, and in every capital they work together more closely and informally than the ambassadors of foreign governments. In every country, except Britain, Commonwealth relations are the responsibility of the Ministries for External Affairs, but in Britain there is still a Commonwealth Relations Office with its own Secretary of State. Prime Ministers' conferences are held every two years or so to consider common problems of major policy; conferences of Ministers concerned with finance, education and other matters are held whenever they are needed; and Ministers and their officials are in touch with one another every day.

Commonwealth governments have also set up a number of councils and committees to co-ordinate their practical activities; they deal with such subjects as economic policy, scientific research, education, shipping and telecommunications. They also co-operate in managing organisations such as the Colombo Plan, under which mutual aid programmes in South East Asia are co-ordinated, the Commonwealth Scholarships Scheme for higher education, under which 1,000 students go to other Commonwealth countries each year, and the Commonwealth Institute in London which teaches people about the Commonwealth. Far more numerous, however, are the links between non-official bodies. Parliaments, the Universities, and many of the professions co-operate through their own Commonwealth associations. Among the most important is the Commonwealth Parliamentary Association to which many members of Commonwealth Parliaments belong; and the educational and technical associations do invaluable work in maintaining common professional standards which enable their degrees and other qualifications to be recognised anywhere in the Commonwealth.

Last, but not least, there is also a great number of learned and voluntary societies such as the Royal Institute of International Affairs, the Royal Commonwealth Society, and the Royal Overseas League, most of which have existed for more than half a century and which have affiliated societies or branches throughout the Commonwealth.

THE COMMONWEALTH AND WORLD AFFAIRS

The Commonwealth does not form a 'third force' in terms of power politics, because each of its governments conducts its own foreign policy quite independently in accordance with its own views and its own interests. The non-aligned nations in Asia and Africa are determined not to be drawn into either the Western or the Soviet bloc, but will accept aid and friendship from both. India believes that, as the world's largest free democracy, she can exercise a powerful influence for peace. The African countries are determined to work together to win for themselves and for the spirit of Africa — sometimes described as the 'African personality' — that important place in world affairs which they feel to be their due.

When Commonwealth governments have 'agreed to disagree'

on international questions they prefer to take their differences into the open forum of the United Nations rather than to establish any system of formal discussion, let alone arbitration, among themselves. In these circumstances, they cannot be expected to speak with one voice in the Assembly of the United Nations, and they do not always do so. The Prime Ministers' conference has, however, done so on two fundamental matters of principle — disarmament and racial equality (which led to the withdrawal from the Commonwealth of South Africa). *The Commonwealth exercises a stable force in the world because its governments, unhampered by the need to present a united political front, feel free to work closely together in so many constructive fields and especially in the all-important task of bridging the gap between the developed and under-developed worlds. This is where the true importance of the Commonwealth lies.*

London, September 1965

The text of this leaflet is based on an article to be published in
The World Book Encyclopaedia

Index

PRINTED IN GREAT BRITAIN BY ROBERT MACLEHOSE AND CO. LTD
THE UNIVERSITY PRESS, GLASGOW